CU01507478

Terry Kilburn is a graduate of Birmingham University, where he was mentored by the late professors E. W. Ives and R. J. Knecht. From Birmingham, he moved to Leicester University's renowned Department of English Local History, gaining an M.A. Terry is also an Associate Fellow of the Royal Historical Society. He has published a popular biography of the Victorian mechanical engineer, Sir Joseph Whitworth, and a number of articles in various academic journals. However, his main passion has always been with Early Modern English and European history, especially that of sixteenth-century England.

"If one looks at something long enough one is sure to see things that everyone else has missed."

– David N Durant

Dedicated to those who are open to alternative ideas, who are prepared to take on board new facts and theories and are ready and willing to adapt to changing narratives. TK

Terry Kilburn

BESS OF HARDWICK:
MYTHS AND REALITIES

AUSTIN MACAULEY PUBLISHERS™

LONDON ∗ CAMBRIDGE ∗ NEW YORK ∗ SHARJAH

Copyright © Terry Kilburn 2024

The right of Terry Kilburn to be identified as author of this work has been asserted by the author in accordance with Sections 77 and 78 of the Copyright, Designs and Patents Act 1988.

All rights reserved. No part of this publication may be reproduced, stored in a retrieval system, or transmitted in any form or by any means, electronic, mechanical, photocopying, recording, or otherwise, without the prior permission of the publishers.

Any person who commits any unauthorised act in relation to this publication may be liable to criminal prosecution and civil claims for damages.

The story, the experiences, and the words are the author's alone.

A CIP catalogue record for this title is available from the British Library.

ISBN 9781035844319 (Paperback)
ISBN 9781035844326 (ePub e-book)

www.austinmacauley.com

First Published 2024
Austin Macauley Publishers Ltd®
1 Canada Square
Canary Wharf
London
E14 5AA

I acknowledge the contributions of the following people who, one way or another, have influenced the work published in this book. My thanks are extended to the Duke of Devonshire KCVO, CBE, the Earl of Strathmore and Kinghorne, Prof. Mark Greengrass, Philip Riden, Peter Foden, Jonathan Mackman, Maureen Taylor, and Paul Gliddon. Special thanks to Lesley Bilby for suggestions and proofreading and to John Barker for drawing my attention to my erratic use of question marks. Thanks also to Vinh Tran and Karen Walker at Austin-Macauley, the staff at the National Archives at Kew, Glasgow Museums, Derbyshire Record Office, National Trust Images, Nottinghamshire Archives, University of Nottingham Manuscripts and Special Collections, and the Borthwick Institute for Archives at York University. My final thanks go to the late professors Eric Ives and 'Bob' Knecht to whom my indebtedness can never be repaid.

Table of Contents

Extract from a nineteenth-century transcript of the Memorandum of Arthur Mower (d. 1610) Woolley collection Brit Mus Add Mss 6671

The old Countess of Shrewsbury departed forth of this world the Saturday being the 13th day of February at Hardwick and was carried to Derby of Tuesday the next after to her tomb there in All Hallows Church and there buried anno dom. 1607 in the fifth year of our most dread Lord King James who was in her time a great purchaser and getter together of much lands and much goods, and was first married to Robert Barley of Barley esq. and then to William Cavendish knight, and then to William Southlow knight captain of the guards, and last to George Talbot earl of Shrewsbury who did surmount her name, she builed Chattesworth, Hardwick, Owlcotts and was a great builder and purchaser.

The old Countess of Shrewsbury departed forth of this world the Saturday being the 13th day of February at Hardwick and was carried to Derby of Tuesday the next after to her tomb there in All Hallows Church and there buried anno dom. 1607[*] in the fifth year of our most dread Lord King James—who was in her time a great purchaser and getter together of much lands and much goods, and was first married to Robert Barley of Barley esq. and then to William Cavendish knight, and then to William Southlow (St Loo) knight captain of the guards, and last to George Talbot, Earl of Shrewsbury who did surmount her name. She builed Chattesworth, Hardwick, Owlcotts and was a great builder and purchaser.

[*]Old Style dating, New Style 1608

Foreword

For anyone seriously interested in Hardwick Hall, this edition of essays and articles is essential reading. Terry Kilburn is passionately interested in and knowledgeable about Hardwick. He worked there for a time as a guide, and this gave him the opportunity of establishing an intimate knowledge of the house and its contents. He is also an original thinker, determined not to accept everything he hears and reads without re-examining the documentary evidence to his own satisfaction and the benefit of the reader.

The short chapter about the Eglantine table, made for Bess of Hardwick and still displayed there, demonstrates the author's scholarship as well as his investigative knowledge. He quickly disproves the widely held idea that this table was commissioned to celebrate three family marriages. I can't wait to go back and have another look at the table, armed with my new knowledge.

Hardwick is a wonderful, fascinating building, and she deserves the close attention of scholars.

Terry Kilburn has certainly played his part in illuminating her history: I urge you to study the fruits of his labours.

Stoker Devonshire
5/4/21
Chatsworth

Introduction

For many, Derbyshire's Elizabethan Hardwick New Hall is the jewel in the crown of the National Trust. Between 2012 and 2015 I was a National Trust 'mansion' volunteer at Hardwick, fulfilling the roles of room guide and tour guide. I met some interesting and wonderful characters among my fellow volunteers. I learned a lot from them.

Late Spring and Summer saw hundreds of visitors to Hardwick's New Hall and some visitors took the time to wander around the remains of the Old Hall. The number of visitors to Hardwick naturally ebbed and flowed according to the time of year. Late Spring and Summer kept 'mansion' volunteers terribly busy, even when much of the time was spent on 'traffic duty' ensuring that visitors followed the designated route. Early and late season, say, up to Easter and from late September, the volume of visitors naturally dwindled. I think all volunteers enjoyed their inter-actions with members of the public, some of whom were truly knowledgeable, others less so.

On quiet days I would spend a good deal of my time pondering everything that was around me, peeping into every nook and cranny discovering things that I found intriguing. In the Long Gallery, for example, I came across graffiti scratched into the stone blocks that make up the great fireplaces. My favourite find was the name Claire Derrie. In the eighteenth century the Derrys were landlords of the nearby Hardwick Inn. Another example was the wall painting hidden behind tapestries on the south wall of the State Withdrawing Room that once stretched right up to the coving of the original ceiling before it was lowered to create rooms above.

My training as a historian told me that some of the things told to visitors somehow did not add up. I expressed my concerns to one of my university mentors who reminded me that most National Trust volunteers at places such as Hardwick though "well-meaning" were not necessarily historians. Most gleaned their knowledge by reading two relatively recent biographies of Bess: David

Durant's *Bess of Hardwick: Portrait of an Elizabethan Dynast* first published in 1977 and Mary S Lovell's *Bess of Hardwick: First Lady of Chatsworth* first published in 2005. Both books are well-written and informative, recommended reading for anyone with an interest in Bess of Hardwick.

The first chapter of this book attempts to shed light on the early sixteenth-century milieu into which Bess and her sisters were born. Chapters 2 is based upon my article 'The Marriage and Wardship of Robert Barley ...' which was published in the *Derbyshire Archaeological Journal* (Vol 134, 2014). A short 'Addendum' to this article was published in 2016 (Vol 136). Here these two articles are updated and combined and additional documents appended including a transcript of Bess's 1546 complaint to Chancery. The discovery of new documentary evidence enabled me to revise what is known about Bess's first marriage to Robert Barley and draw attention to the previously unknown role played by Peter Freschevile in Robert's wardship and marriage together with the consequences this had for Bess as she sought to pursue her claims for dower. At the time they were writing neither Durant nor Lovell were aware of the role of Peter Freschevile in Robert Barley's wardship and his marriage to Bess. Consequently, there is no mention of this in their books.

My article 'Sir William Cavendish: Marriage to Bess ...' was published in the *Derbyshire Archaeological Journal* (Vol 139, 2019) and forms the basis of chapter 3 which, by placing his actions in the context of the political and religious upheavals of the mid-sixteenth century, seeks to provide new explanations for Sir William's marriage to Bess and his subsequent move to Derbyshire.

'Three Into Two Won't Go...' was published in the Derbyshire Archaeological Society's *Derbyshire Miscellany* (Vol 21: Part 2, 2016) and seeks to show that Hardwick's famous 'Eglantine Table' does not represent three marriages. Bess's story, and that of the hall she built, is somewhat bedevilled by such inaccuracies and myths old and new. As recently as 2016 an intarsia panel depicting the Round City of Baghdad with its mosque and Caliph's palace has been mis-identified as Solomon's Temple (*Hardwick Hall, A Great Old Castle of Romance*, National Trust, 2016, pages 16 and 106). A long-standing myth is that Bess's corpse lay in state in the High Great Chamber for some three months before her funeral was held at Derby. Early on in my four-season stint as a room and tour guide at Hardwick I was told by a veteran volunteer that this was because Bess died in February when the winter weather was not conducive for a ceremonial burial. The reality tells a quite different story. Not all myths are old ones. Some modern authors have argued that Bess was born in 1527 but, here again, the available evidence indicates a different reality. The jury is still out as to whether the band of undressed stonework around the exterior of the hall is evidence of the original colonnades being left unfinished or – a more likely reality – of their partial removal in the seventeenth century.

Henry Marmion always appeared to me to be a somewhat shadowy character, but one strongly associated with the Hardwicks. He was an executor of John Hardwick's will and three generations of his family appear to have served Bess in one capacity or other. Chapter six explores this relationship further. It is likely the result of Henry Marmion's connection to the Hardwicks that Bess first entered the service of an aristocratic family and commenced a journey that led her to the title Countess of Shrewsbury.

In 2014 the National Trust focused the attention of visitors to Hardwick on the story of Bess's granddaughter, Arbella Stuart. Volunteers set about reading David Durant's 1978 *Arbella Stuart: A Rival to the Queen* and perhaps Sarah Gristwood's 2003 *Arbella: England's Lost Queen*. Few, if any, skimmed through Ruth Norrington's *In the Shadow of the Throne* (2002). It occurred to me that a 'quick fix' was needed and so I set about writing a brief self-published biography of Arbella, *Hardwick's Royal Princess…*, which, as chapter 7, is reproduced and updated in this book.

The book ends with an epilogue: a brief assessment of my Bess. Has she been mis-represented by successive authors? Was she a scheming vixen, a consummate manipulator of four husbands, a woman determined to build a dynasty? To what extent was she manipulated by others? Has she been credited for things which rightly should be credited to others? Was she a proto-feminist, a woman 'ahead of her time' or was she more simply a woman 'of her time'?

The Appendix seeks to build on the work of Alistair Laing whose 1989 article, 'Rechristenings at Hardwick', *Country Life*, 183, (9 Mar 1989), 134-5, drew readers' attention to a number of mis-identified portraits at Hardwick Hall. Among other observations, it is argued here that one of the mis-identified portraits at Hardwick is, in fact, a 'lost' portrait of Sir Thomas More.

This book is not a conventional biography of Bess of Hardwick. It brings together in a single volume some of my research undertaken during the last seven years or so. Academic journals tend not to favour long and detailed footnotes. I have chosen to include detailed footnotes where appropriate as they contain a good deal of additional information which augments that included in the main text. Many printed works and original sources are cited in footnotes together with unpublished primary material and additional analytical content. Note that the prefix TNA refers to original documents housed at the National Archive at Kew. This edition is also blessed with an extensive index.

It is perhaps inevitable that new ideas meet resistance. It can be hard to accept something that challenges what we think we know. For some, the easy way out is to seek comfort in the notion that unless what is said concurs with better-known authors it can be readily dismissed. Some will find elements of this book challenging, perhaps controversial, even heretical, but my hope is that it will in a small way help to eliminate some of the prevailing mythology and inaccuracies that continue to distort the Bess of Hardwick narrative. The work is dedicated to those Hardwick volunteers who are open to alternative ideas, prepared to take onboard new facts and theories, and ready and willing to adapt to changing narratives.

1. The Early Years of Bess and Her Sisters

The earliest known portrait of Bess. c1560
© National Trust Images/Angelo Hornak

Little is known of the early lives of John Hardwick's children. Although Bess would end her life as the Dowager Countess of Shrewsbury, there is very little contemporary evidence relating to the childhoods of Bess and her siblings. Nonetheless, despite the paucity of evidence, it is possible to piece together some picture of the early years of the lives of the Hardwick children.

The north-east Derbyshire milieu into which John Hardwick's children were born consisted of mainly minor gentry and 'gentlemen-yeomen' farmers. The death of the powerful William, Lord Hastings, in 1483 left something of a power vacuum such that there was no aristocratic magnate exercising control over much of the county[1]. This role fell to the earls of Shrewsbury. George, 4th Earl of

Shrewsbury, was one of the two supervisors of John Hardwick's will.[2] The whole of Derbyshire could boast only a handful of knights including the Leakes of Sutton Scarsdale, the leading north-east Derbyshire gentry family.[3]

There were families, like the Hardwicks, who acquired Coats of Arms in the fifteenth century but due to the high cost of office holding and military charges chose to pay a fine and be in distraint of knighthood. Families, such as the Frescheviles, went on to acquire the rank of knighthood in the next century. Others, like the Hardwicks, remained in the lowest rank of the armigerous gentry, the esquires. Many of these families, including the Leakes, Linacres, Frescheviles, Markhams, Foljambes, Charworths, Merrings, Barleys, and Hardwicks, were related and interrelated by marriage. For example, John Hardwick's wife, Elizabeth, was the daughter of Thomas Leake's second son Sir William Leake of Sutton Scarsdale. Thomas's sister Catherine married Sir Godfrey Foljambe and his sister Elizabeth married John Freschevile, together parents of Sir Peter Freschevile. The male members of these families were often involved in local administration and tax collection, and some presided over local courts.

The Hardwick estate was not a manor, it was a freehold property part of the manor of Stainsby. Its origins date back to the early thirteen century. By the late fourteenth century, it was in the hands of Roger and Joan Hardwick. The estate was relatively small. Following the death of John Hardwick in 1528 an Inquisition Post-Mortem held at Wirksworth on 20 October recorded that his estate comprised:

> *a messuage and 60 acres of arable land, 60 acres of pasture and 10 acres of meadow in 'le Heth'*
> *a close in Hardwick called 'le Oxclose'*
> *two closes in Hardwick called 'Hareleyez'*
> *a close in Hardwick called 'le Nether Throwcrofte' with 'le spryng' called 'le Netherestwood'*
> *a close in Hardwick called 'le Middilfeld'*
> *a close in Hardwick called 'Overeswood'*
> *a capital messuage called 'Herdwekehall' with appurtenances within the lordship of Steynysby in Derbyshire*
> *100 acres of arable land, 100 acres of pasture, 100 acres of wood and 15 acres of meadow in Hardwick*

2 messuages, 60 acres of arable land, 80 acres of pasture, and 10 acres of meadow in 'Heth'.

10 acres of arable land and 10 acres of pasture in Glapwell.

40 acres of pasture, 20 acres of arable land and 10 acres of wood in Owlecottes.

By his charter dated 6 January 19 Henry VIII [1528], John Hardweke, amongst other things, gave all these lands, as his manors of Hardwick and 'Heth', except those lands in which he and Elizabeth were jointly seised, to Edward Willoughby, knight, John Leek, esquire, Henry Marmyon, esquire, Thomas Leek, gentleman, Robert Perot, clerk, and Ralph Spalton, yeoman, all now surviving, and Edward Bareford, now deceased, to hold for the implementation of his will. [4]

A further IPM held in August 1529 found that John held Hardwick Hall, of Sir John Savage, together with lands in Heath and Ault Hucknall valued at £132 15s 4d per annum.[5] John's income derived largely from rents and the resources of his holdings. His son James enlarged the estate. By 1580, it was valued at some £390 but this was at great financial cost to himself, James died bankrupt in Fleet Prison in 1580/1. It was left to John Hardwick's grandson, William, to add significantly to the size and value of the estate after he acquired it in 1583.[6]

John's daughters had a great deal to offer their prospective husbands' households. Examples of her handwriting demonstrate that their mother wrote in a clear hand. She would also have been numerate.[7] She would have been the person responsible for running the day-to-day affairs of the family. It was her job to prepare her daughters for their roles as wives by providing them with the skills required to run their own future households.

In addition to literacy and numeracy, the type of education given typically to girls of Hardwick's rank would focus on all aspects of household management such as compiling the account books, handling servants, baking, brewing, sewing, needlework, embroidery, spinning, some knowledge of the growing and use of herbs for both medicinal use and for cooking, together with a wide range of other domestic duties. It has often been assumed that Bess acquired her accounting skills from Sir William Cavendish but that does not seem to have been the case. As is shown in Cavendish's accounts for 1548-50, compiled mainly by Bess, the accounting skills Bess showed in later life were already present by the time she married Cavendish in 1547.[9]

In his will dated 9 January 1528, John Hardwick placed his soul in the hands of God, St Mary and all the Holy Company of Saints.[10] He was a catholic and his children would have been brought up in the catholic faith. Bess would eventually encounter evangelical Protestantism via Sir William Cavendish and most likely the Greys of Bradgate, together with other members of a significant protestant affinity, including the Willoughbys, headed by Henry Grey.[11]

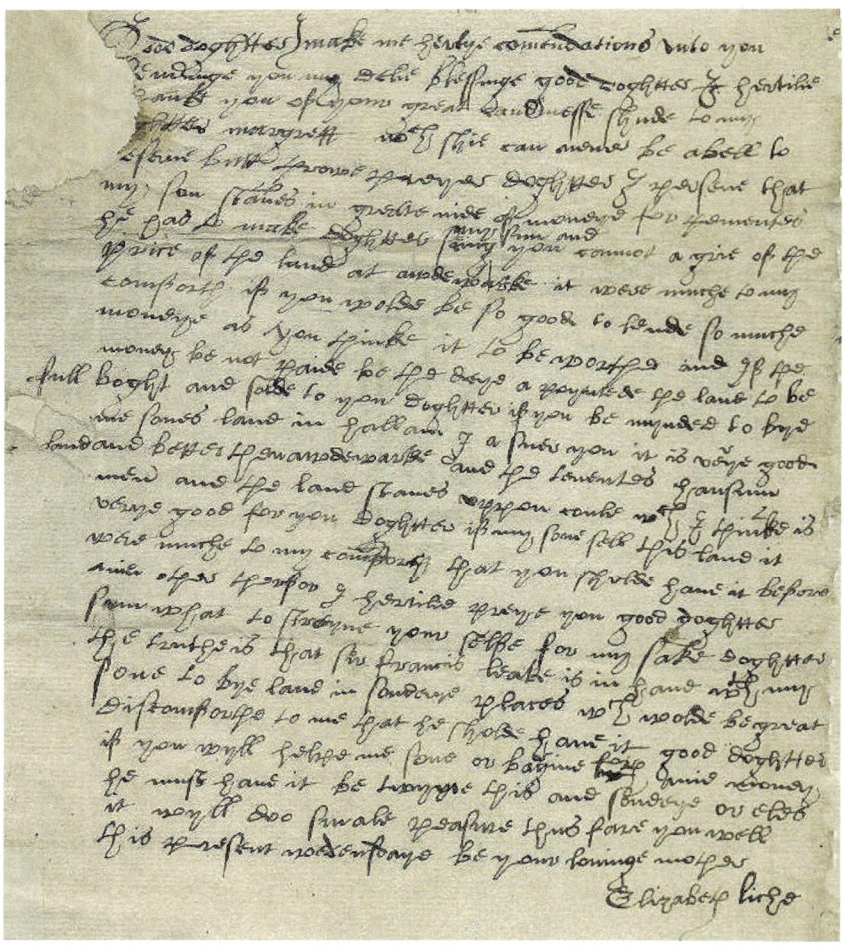

Bess's mother's handwriting, c 1565
MSS, X,d. (48), Folger-Shakespeare Library

Cavendish accounts, 1548-50, compiled by Bess (see n9)
MSS,.X.d.486 Folger-Shakespeare Library

In an unsuccessful attempt to minimise the impact wardship would have on his son's inheritance, John Hardwick placed much of his estate in the hands of feoffees (trustees) for a period of 20 years. John's five daughters - Alice, Elizabeth, Dorothy, Jane, and Mary - were all alive in early January 1528 when their father's will was made. He placed them in the custody of their mother until they reached the age of 15, and she was to have 26s 8d per year (2 marks) for food and drink for each of them from his executors, Henry Marmion and their mother's uncle, John Leake, whose advice, and counsel they were to follow. They were each to receive a relatively modest marriage portion of a minimum of 40 marks, more if the estate could afford it. Should any of them die unmarried, their portion was to be divided equally between the survivors. Their marriage portions were their share of their father's estate. To put this into perspective, the average amount of dowry provided by knights to their daughters during this period was between 200-300 marks.[12]

John's wife was also well provided for in her husband's will. She was to have the hall with the demesne lands pertaining to it for 20 years, during her widowhood, paying the executors 14 marks per year. Elizabeth's widowhood didn't last very long. In or about 1529, she married Ralph Leche of Chatsworth, and as a result, she became subject to the rules of coverture. Bess's first appearance in the historical record appears to have been when aged 7 along with her sisters Alice 10, Dorothy 9 (if born in 1519, or 5 if born in 1523), Jane 2, and Mary up to 12 months, as one of the five unnamed daughters provided for by their father's will.

Elizabeth Leake's marriage to John Hardwick produced six children: five girls and the all-important male heir. However, modern biographies of Bess tend to skip Bess and her siblings' early years and the order of their births has been the subject of much debate. Bess's modern biographers tend to present a traditional, though very inaccurate, account of her first marriage to Robert Barley.[13] They quickly arrive at her second marriage to Sir William Cavendish. In 1549, he gave Bess a book set with gold and precious stones which contained a portrait of each of them.[14]

However, the earliest portrait we have of Bess dates from c1560 and is said to depict her in her early thirties. At that time, she would have been married to Sir William St Loe. But the dating of this portrait is suspect because it assumes that Bess was born in 1527. However, if, as will be argued here, Bess was born in 1521 the portrait would then date to c1553 when she was married to Sir William Cavendish. We have no portraits of Bess or her siblings that date to their younger years.

Prior to the 1970s, the year of Bess's birth was generally accepted as c1520 but several recent biographies state she was born in 1527 which has led to a good deal of confusion over the birth order of John Hardwick's children.[15] The notion of Bess being born in 1527 seems to have more to do with a desire to have her moving into Hardwick New Hall on her alleged seventieth birthday than it has to do with any credible historical evidence. Although an entry in the Hardwick household accounts for the 4 October 1597 records a payment of 20 shillings to three of Bess's servants who played music when she moved into the new hall, there is no mention of the occasion having been her birthday, seventieth or otherwise.[16]

There can be no dispute when it comes to the year of birth of John Hardwick's son, James. After his father's death, he became a ward of court and his wardship was sold to John Bugby, a minor court official, who was expelled from Hardwick by John Hardwick's executors in 1533.[17] James entered into his inheritance when he reached the age of 21, that is in 1546 which places the year of his birth as 1525.

The relatively modern notion that Bess was born in 1527 appears to be predicated on the basis that 16 was the age of maturity.[18] However, in the sixteenth century 16 was not recognised as being an age of passage in either Common or Canon Law. The legal age of majority was 21 for males and females although female wards entered their inheritances at the age of 14.[19] The first time the age of 16 took on any legal significance was in 1929 when the Age of Marriage Act raised the age at which boys and girls could marry with the consent of their parents or guardians from 14 to 16. The 2023 Marriage and Civil Partnership (Minimum Age) Act has raised the minimum age for marriage to 18 in England and Wales.

Until 1753, a marriage ceremony could take place anywhere provided it was conducted by an ordained minister and independently witnessed. If 16 was the age of maturity in the sixteenth century why in his will would John Hardwick only provide for his daughters' upkeep until they reached the age of 15? He may well have expected that his daughters would all have been espoused and contracted to marry by that age. In Bess's case, that provision would have run out in 1536, the year Ralph purchased Robert Barley's wardship and Bess and Robert were espoused.[20]

In his *Bess of Hardwick: Portrait of an Elizabethan Dynast*, David Durant argued that the youngest of John's daughters was Alice and that Mary and Jane were older than Bess. He did not account for Dorothy who was certainly living in 1528 when her father made his will but is not mentioned thereafter.[21] Mary Lovell in her *Bess of Hardwick: First Lady of Chatsworth*, argues that John had two daughters who died prior to Mary Hardwick's birth. She gives the birth order of John's surviving daughters as Mary (c1523) Jane (c1524), Elizabeth (Bess,

1527) and Alice (1528).[22] Again, there is no mention of Dorothy, presumably for Lovell she was one of the two daughters who died before 1523 but that is very unlikely.

As we have seen, John Hardwick's will makes it clear that he had five daughters living at the time of his death, not four. Dorothy was most likely one of the five and perhaps died shortly after her father. There was some uncertainty in John's will regarding whether or not his wife was pregnant. She wasn't. Neither John nor his wife could have known the gender of an unborn child, but had she given birth that child would have been a second son or a sixth daughter.

There is a document in the Belvoir Castle archive which, on the face of it, would appear to support a view of the birth order of John Hardwick's children with Mary shown as the eldest. It is an anonymous roughly drawn pedigree of 'Leeke, Grey, and Freschevile' dating from c1565[23] which lists the surviving children of John Hardwick in this order: Mary (not actually named, identified as the wife of Wingfield), Jane, James, Elizabeth, Alice (incorrectly named as Anna). However, this may be the result of how the lineages are being read. At first sight, reading from left to right, it appears to list John Hardwick's children beginning with Mary, thereby implying to modern eyes at least that she was the eldest of John's children.

Belvoir Castle MSS, hand-drawn pedigree c1565

However, the evidence we have suggests that Mary was the youngest, not the eldest. It may well be that the compiler began with Mary not because she was the oldest but because she was the youngest and the birth order is intended to be read from left to right commencing with Mary as the youngest. Although highly unlikely, the somewhat unreliable hand-drawn Belvoir pedigree is the only one to imply that James and the incorrectly named Alice were born at the same time, i.e. that they were twins. If accurate, this would, of course, leave ample room for the birth of Dorothy. It would also allow for Mary and Jane alone to be residents at Hardwick by 1540. However, the fact that Mary is not listed by name and Alice is named as Anna could be said to cast a good degree of doubt on the compiler's accuracy.

Establishing the birth order of John Hardwick's daughters is problematic. In a Chancery case begun c1546, Jane Hardwick's husband Godfrey Boswell listed John's daughters as Mary, Elizabeth, Alice, Dorothy and Jane.[24] He was suing for an unpaid marriage portion and most likely named his wife last as she was the object of his proceedings. Dorothy is listed in only one copy of the visitations, as the youngest of the daughters.[25] The published version of the 1569 Herald's visitation of Derbyshire lists Hardwick's daughters as Jane, Mary, Elizabeth and Alice.[26]

In a 1615 copy of the 1569 visitation, they are listed as Mary, Jane, Alice and Elizabeth.[27] In an earlier written account, the daughters are listed as Alice, Elizabeth, Mary and Jane.[28] In the published version of the 1569 visitation, Alice and Mary are placed before their brother, James, but in the two manuscript copies of the visitation, Elizabeth and Jane are placed before James. Both these hand-written pedigrees pair Alice with Elizabeth and Mary with Jane. Only the published version of the 1569 visitation pairs the daughters differently, but this appears to be the result of how the printed page was formatted. Dorothy does not appear in the Belvoir Castle manuscript pedigree where Mary is paired with Jane and Elizabeth with Alice.[29]

Alice	Dorothy	Elizabeth	James	Jane	Mary
b1518	b1519?	b1521	b1525	b1525/6	b1527
	or 1523/4?				

Likely birth order of John Hardwick's children

The first of John Hardwick's daughters to be married appears to have been Alice. Ralph Leche was the legal guardian of his nephew, Francis Leche. Ralph most likely contracted Alice's espousal to his nephew sometime around her 15th birthday c1533, which would have coincided with the ending of the provision made for her upkeep in her father's will. Her husband Francis was born on 1 November 1525 and would not have reached the age of 14, the age at which he could consent to marriage, until November 1539. Francis's 1548 decision to sell his land was the result of Alice's 'lewd life'. She had committed adultery and Thomas Seymour, acting on behalf of Thomas Agard, informed his brother Edward, Lord Protector, that Francis would sooner 'give (his land) to any man

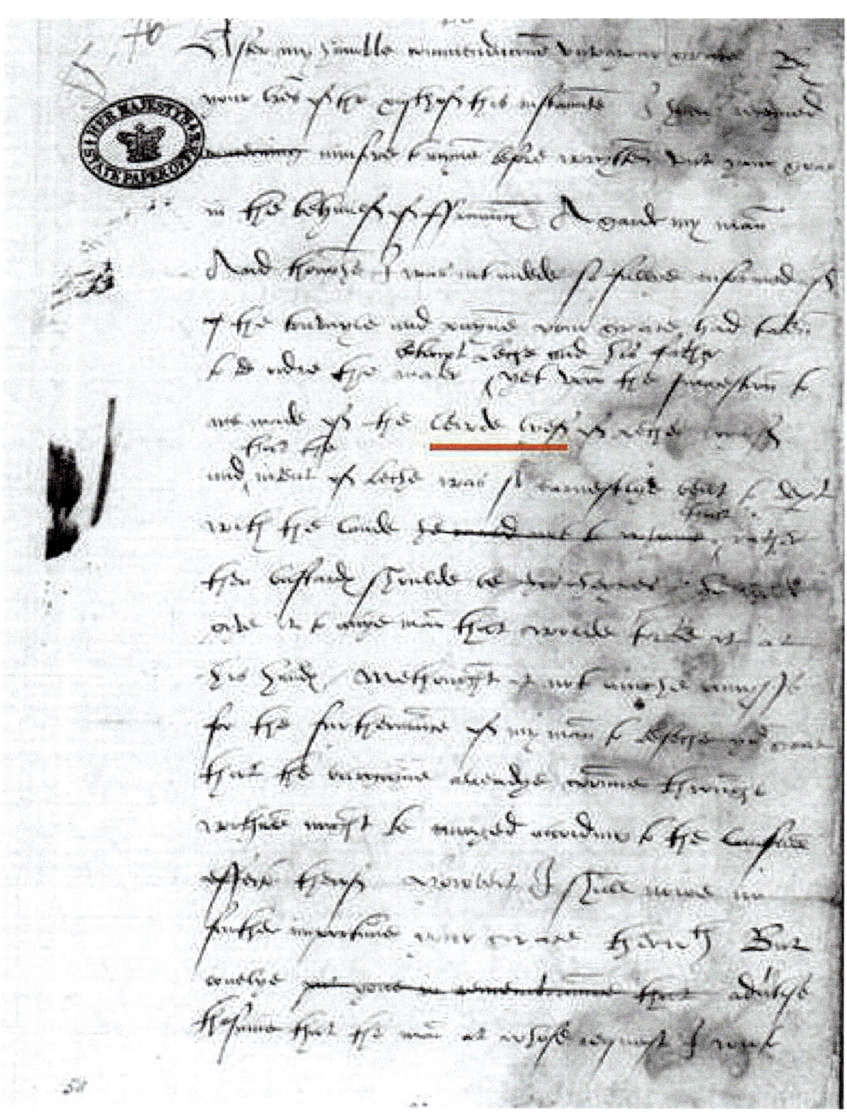

Letter dated 19 Aug 1548 from Thomas Seymour to his brother Edward, Lord Protector, in reference to Alice's 'lewd life'
© The National Archive C1/651/13

that would take it' rather than see it inherited by 'bastards' (illegitimate children).[30] Thomas Agard purchased the manors of Chatsworth and Cromford and his son, Francis Agard, sold the two manors to Sir William Cavendish who granted jointure to Bess.

The next of John Hardwick's daughters to marry was Bess. In 1536, Ralph Leche purchased the wardship and marriage of Robert Barley, the eldest son and heir of near neighbour, Arthur Barley of Barley Lees, to whom Bess was espoused.[31] It was not uncommon for a wardship to be sold to ease the burden of debt. In 1538, weighed down by debt and finding himself to be an inmate in the Fleet, Ralph sold Robert's wardship and marriage to Henry Marmion.[32] In the sixteenth century, it was normal for girls who were espoused to go and live in the household of the groom, or the couple might join the bride's household.

Some, depending on their age, might remain in their natal home. Where an espoused couple would live would be specified in the marriage contract agreed between their respective fathers or guardians.[33] In the summer of 1540, Jane and Mary were the only two of John Hardwick's daughters known to have been living at Hardwick which may also be another indicator pointing to the conclusion that Jane and Mary were the youngest of Hardwick's daughters.[34]

Robert Barley was born in 1530 and so would have been around 6 years old when the marriage contract, or bargain, was agreed between Ralph and Arthur Barley.[35] If Bess had been born in 1527, she would have been around 9 years of age. Ecclesiastical or Canon law held that for a female to consent to marriage she had to be 12 years of age, a boy 14 years of age.[36] In this case, both Robert and Bess appear to have been of 'tender years' and 'within age', i.e. under 21, at the time of their espousal. However, was Bess really born in 1527?

There is a substantial amount of evidence which indicates that Bess was most likely born c1521 rather than 1527. As a widow, Bess would have been deemed a *femme sole* which gave certain legal rights not permitted to a married woman, or *femme covert*.[37] Indeed, widows were in a relatively strong position *vis-a-vis* spinsters or married women. They retained their goods and chattels from their marriages and could protect their inheritances via prenuptial agreements. As a widow, Bess had the right to sue in the law courts as sole plaintiff on condition that she was 21 or over.

In 1545, a few months after the December 1544 death of her husband, Robert, Bess sued Peter Freschevile, guardian of Robert's younger brother and natural heir, George Barley, for her Barley dower in the Court of Common Pleas. Eighteen months later she switched her case to the prerogative Court of Chancery. In both courts, she sued as sole plaintiff.[38] Had Bess been under 21 she would have been represented by her guardian, Ralph Leche, or possibly by Henry Marmion. Furthermore, Freschevile was related to the Hardwicks and had Bess been under 21 when she began legal proceedings against him, he would have had a very good idea of her age and would have instructed his attorney to lodge an objection. He didn't.

Some of the confusion surrounding Bess's year of birth has been caused by the Duchess of Newcastle's 1667 comment that both Bess and Robert were of 'tender years', i.e. under the age of 21, when they married. Indeed, in 1546 Bess herself informed Chancery that she and Robert were of 'tender years' at the time of their espousal. According to law when a couple were espoused, unless coercion had been used, they were deemed to be married. However, the marriage bargain was not complete until the marriage ceremony had taken place and the marriage consummated.[39]

Bess and Robert may well have been quite young when their marriage was contracted in 1536. Bess would have been around 15, Robert then aged 6, both under 21. The fact is that during this period marriage contracts frequently involved two people whose ages were many years apart. It cannot be assumed that the marriage ceremony of Robert and Bess took place at the same time as the espousal. We do not know if Robert and Bess consummated their marriage, we do know it produced no issue.

When Godfrey Boswell purchased Robert's wardship in 1544, he was at pains to stress and have the clerk record, that Robert was 14 when his father died, that is, the age at which he could legally consent to marriage. To limit the impact wardship would have on Arthur Barley's estate, it was in Boswell's interest to have it recorded that Robert was legally married *before* his father's death. In fact, Robert, born in January 1530, did not reach the age of 14 until *after* his father died on 28 May 1543 which means that his marriage to Bess took place at a time when, according to Canon Law, Robert could not give his consent to marriage. Indeed, Arthur Barley's IPM, dated 25 October 1543, states that Robert was then 'aged 13 years, 10 months and 2 days.'

In effect, Robert's marriage to Bess could have been deemed invalid, something that must have been at the forefront of Boswell's mind when he sought to purchase Robert's wardship from the Court of Wards.[40] However, the extent to which Boswell's statement of Robert's age can be taken as reliable evidence of the timing of his marriage to Bess is open to question. What, exactly, did Boswell mean by married?

Today, marriage begins on the wedding day at the time the marriage ceremony takes place. In the sixteenth century, the mean age at first marriage for women in Bess's social rank was around 25.[41] The marriage process began at espousal but was not complete until the marriage ceremony had taken place and the marriage consummated. The act of consummation normally took place in front of witnesses within hours of the marriage ceremony.

On the other hand, there could be many years between the spousal contract and the marriage ceremony. The evidence suggests that the first stage of marriage, in this case the spousal contract for Robert's marriage to Bess, was agreed between Arthur Barley and Ralph Leche in 1536, clearly within the lifetime of Robert's father. Is this what Boswell meant by 'married', i.e. was he referring to the date of Robert and Bess's spousal contract?

The second stage of their marriage contract, Robert and Bess's wedding ceremony, probably took place at Barley Lees, possibly in haste, shortly before Arthur Barley died. Within days of his father's death, Robert was taken from Barley Lees. Sir Peter Freschevile of Staveley immediately launched legal proceedings against Ralph Leche, Bess's mother, and Henry Marmion, alleging that they had forcibly abducted Robert from Barley Lees. Freschevile claimed that he was Robert's legal guardian and, as such, he alone had the right to determine Robert's marriage.

Thus, as he had not consented to it, Robert's marriage to Bess was illegal.[42] Robert's death in December 1544 brought an end to these proceedings, but Freschevile continued to maintain that Robert's marriage to Bess was illegal and refused to pay Bess a widow's dower. This led to Bess commencing legal proceedings against George Barley, Robert's younger brother and heir, and Peter Freschevile George's undisputed legal guardian. Eventually, following a lengthy legal battle in both Common and prerogative courts, Bess did receive her modest Barley dower which was paid for the rest of her life.[43]

The plaque on Bess's monument in Derby Cathedral states that she was 87 when she died on 13 February 1608 thus indicating that 1521 was the year of her birth. Some object that the information on the plaque cannot be trusted because it refers to her grandson as 'Duke of Newcastle' which he did not become until 1655, 47 years after her death. However, all this shows is that in order to convey her grandson's elevation a new plaque probably replaced an original one. The information regarding Bess's age at death given on the new plaque would simply have been copied from the original.

On his 52nd birthday, in November 1604, Gilbert Talbot wrote a letter to Robert Cecil in which he informed Cecil that Bess, who he described as his 'unkind mother-in-law', was then about 84 years of age.[44] Had Bess moved into Hardwick New Hall on her 70th birthday, as has been claimed by those seeking to set her birth year as 1527, Gilbert would surely have been aware of the fact and would therefore have thought her to have been around 77 in late 1604, not about 84. Clearly, members of Bess's own family held that she was born in or around 1521, not 1527. This also confirms that, as stated on the monument plaque, Bess was indeed 87 years of age when she died in 1608. As one historian recently observed, 'modern biographers have tied themselves into ridiculous knots trying to give Bess a birth date of 1527, but the best contemporary evidence is clear and consistent pointing to 1521 as her most likely year of birth'.[45]

The evidence we have suggests that Alice and Bess were born before James, Jane, and Mary. Dorothy, possibly born between 1518 and 1521 or, between 1522 and 1524, would have been no older than 10 when her father died in 1528 and possibly as young as 4. She is not listed in the herald's visitations and appears to have died by the mid-1540s. In 1536, Bess's marriage portion was 40 marks which suggests that Dorothy was still alive in that year because if she had died before that date in accordance with their father's will the marriage portions of his surviving daughters would have been in excess of 40 marks.

The arms of Boswell impaling Hardwick, Old Manor, Brampton en le Morthen, South Yorkshire. Photograph author

Jane Hardwick was probably born in 1527 and was the third of John Hardwick's daughters to marry. The exact year of her marriage to Godfrey Boswell is unknown but the most likely date for their espousal was probably in 1542/3 with the marriage ceremony taking place in or around 1545. Members of the Tudor gentry commonly sent their daughters to live in another household, preferably one of higher rank than their own. This is known as the 'placing-out' or 'putting out' system.[46] According to a 1545/6 legal action taken by her husband, Godfrey Boswell, Jane was at some point 'put out' 'in the service of Lady Carowe, wife of Sir George Carowe, knight'.[47] As captain of the ill-fated *Mary Rose*, Sir George went to his death on 19 July 1545. The Carews were among those West Country families associated with the Grey affinity. Some members of the Carew family supported Jane Grey's abortive rule and, along with Henry Grey, George's brother, Sir Peter Carew, was one of the principals of the Wyatt Rebellion. It is possible that Jane Hardwick's service with the Carew's may have stemmed from this connection, i.e. that it may have been initiated by Marmion via the Willoughbys of Wollaton or the Greys of Bradgate.

Probably with the usual degree of exaggeration, Boswell claimed that together with Ralph Leche, John Hardwick's executors Henry Marmion and John Leake, had embezzled hundreds of pounds which ought to have been paid to Hardwick's daughters. This may have included Dorothy's marriage portion which was to be shared by Hardwick's other daughters following Dorothy's death. Marmion had given a payment of £15 for Jane's apparel when she was in service to Lady Carew but Boswell alleged that nothing else had been paid to any of John Hardwick's daughters. John Leake died at this time and Boswell had to renew his legal proceedings with Marmion as the sole defendant. Apart from this payment of £15 we know nothing of Jane Hardwick's service with Lady Carew.

In his proceedings, Boswell referred to a period when 'as such time as Jane was' in service to Lady Carew, the second wife of Sir George Carew, but does not say exactly when this was. On the other hand, he does not describe Lady Carew as a widow and therefore Jane must have been in Lady Carew's service before July 1545. In the autumn of 1540, Sir George married his second wife, Mary, daughter of the unfortunate Sir Henry Norris who was executed as one of the men with whom Queen Anne Boleyn allegedly committed adultery. This would have been the Lady Carew to whom Jane was 'put out'. It may be that

Jane entered Mary Carew's service around late 1540, or shortly thereafter, and left before Sir George's death in July 1545, possibly in 1542 when, on the death of his father, 23-year-old Godfrey Boswell entered into his inheritance, the same year, in fact, that Jane would have reached the age of 15 and the funding provided for her upkeep in her father's will would have ceased. They had one son who died without issue and four daughters who all married into the local gentry.

Boswell's legal action was not the only time that Henry Marmion's relations with John Hardwick's daughters resulted in his being brought before the courts. As stated previously, we know for sure that Jane and her sister, Mary, were residing at Hardwick in 1540. At the beginning of August 1540, Henry Marmion was alleged to have organised an attack on Chatsworth for which he, Bess's mother and others were brought before the Derby assizes and were later investigated by Star Chamber.[48] John Wykes claimed that Roger Leche had enfeoffed lands at Chatsworth to the use of his wife Anne for her lifetime, with reversion to Roger's son Francis Leche after Anne's death. Wykes married Anne in 1536.

He alleged that around six o'clock on the morning of 2 August 1540, Henry Marmion, his servant Nicholas Waterhouse, Edmund Plattes, who was Jane Hardwick's servant, and John Wild, of Hardwick, yeoman, together with a dozen or more 'evil-disposed and riotous persons', launched an armed attack on Langley Close at Chatsworth, assaulted Anne Wykes and Mary Hone, and then drove off with three cartloads of wheat sheaves. When questioned in Star Chamber, Wild, Waterhouse and Plattes all denied charges of riotous or unlawful assembly, forcible entry, assault, or battery.

At harvest time, Jane and Mary ordered John Wild and Edmund Plattes to cut the crops and Marmion instructed Waterhouse to deliver them to Hardwick which, they stated, they did in a peaceful manner. Wykes claimed that during the attack his wife's head was 'broken' and that one of the defendants left behind a wood knife and other weapons. At the Derby assizes, the defendants repeated their claim that they had not behaved riotously. They also stated that in an effort to reach some kind of settlement Wykes and Anne went to Hardwick to see Jane and Mary. The two sisters refused to accept any kind of agreement and instead arranged for the defendants to carry away the crops.

The defendants agreed that they had been paid for their services by Henry Marmion and Jane and Mary Hardwick. Jane and Mary were not indicted, possibly because at that time they would have been in their early teens. The documents relating to the Langley Close incident make it clear that Henry Marmion was acting only on behalf of Jane and Mary. There is no mention of Bess throughout. So where was she? One plausible explanation could be that by this time she was residing with the Barleys at Barley Lees.

The last of John Hardwick's surviving daughters, Mary, is sometimes referred to as 'of Brampton'. This may indicate that at some point after 1536 she may have resided with Boswell and her sister, Jane. Mary was the only one of John's daughters whose first marriage was not to a family belonging to the local gentry. In early May 1545, aged 18, she married Richard Wingfield, son of Sir Anthony Wingfield, in London. Like Sir William Cavendish, Sir Anthony was an agent of Thomas Cromwell and a client of Edward Seymour. He became a Privy Councillor in Henry VIII's reign. The two men would have known each other well. Richard and Mary had five children, four sons and two daughters. Their son Anthony became a renowned scholar, and tutor to Charles Cavendish's sons, Bess's grandsons Charles and William, by his second wife, Catherine Ogle. Between 1558 and 1571 Richard's sister, Anne Wingfield, served at Elizabeth I's court as a Lady of the Privy Chamber.[49]

Sir Richard Wingfield, husband of Mary Hardwick, portrait dated 1587
© Phillip Mould Images

In or about 1562, Elizabeth Leche, second daughter of Ralph Leche, half-sister to the Hardwick children, married Richard Wingfield's younger brother, another Anthony (c1535 to c1593). For thirty-four years, he held the important office of gentleman usher at the court of Queen Elizabeth and often corresponded with Bess and the Earl of Shrewsbury. In 1589, he was intended to accompany Bess's son, Henry Cavendish, on a trip to Turkey but his place was

Close-up of the central section of the 1587 portrait of
Sir Richard Wingfield depicting the Hardwick Arms

taken by Richard Mallory who had trading interests in the country. Anthony's wife, Elizabeth, was held in high esteem by the Queen and served as the Mother of the Maids in 1591 and 1597.[50] In this role, she was responsible for the conduct and welfare of the young Maids of Honour at Elizabeth's court. There were normally six Maids of Honour at any one time and, other than in cases of misconduct, kept their posts until they married.[51] She kept in close contact with her half-sister, Bess, keeping her informed of the goings-on at court and advising on New Years gifts. Indeed, she was arguably much closer to the Queen than Bess. The other two Leche half-sisters, Jane and Margaret, both married well. They followed the usual route and were espoused to gentlemen from the local area. Jane married Thomas Kniveton and Margaret married twice, firstly to a so-far unidentified man named Harrison and secondly to Richard Slater. [52]

The most likely order of the births of John Hardwick's children appears to be Alice, Dorothy, Elizabeth, James, Jane, and Mary. The key to this is the fact that Ralph Leche was unwilling to meet the expense of paying for the upkeep of his wife's daughters from her first marriage to John Hardwick once the provisions John had made for them in his will expired. As noted above, it was common practice for young girls to move into the households of the person they were espoused to marry.

In the cases of Alice, Bess, and Jane, the onset of their 15th birthdays, the age when their father's provisions for their upkeep were due to end, seems to have been the catalyst for espousal bargains. The only exception to this is with John's youngest daughter, Mary. It was usually the women of the household that arranged marriages for their children, although Mary's 1545 marriage to Richard Wingfield took place when Bess was probably in service to the Greys and may have owed more to Sir William Cavendish's friendship with Sir Anthony Wingfield than it did to Bess.

When 15-year-old Bess was espoused to Robert Barley in 1536 she could not in her wildest dreams have imagined that some three decades later she would marry George Talbot and enter the ranks of the English aristocracy as the Countess of Shrewsbury. She was the only child of John and Elizabeth Hardwick to attain such heights. But, nevertheless, she would remain deeply rooted in the family nexuses of north-east Derbyshire into which she was born in 1521.

Chapter 1: Appendix
Summarized Last Will and Testament of John Hardwick

Will, dated 9 January 1528, of John Herdweke of Hardwick. He grants his soul to god, St Mary and all the holy company. Body to be buried in the church of Hawthuknall (Ault Hucknall), in the arch between the chancel and the new aisle. Best beast to the vicar for his mortuary, with bread, ale and wax and other funeral expenses at the discretion of his executors. To the mother churches of St Mary, Coventry and St Chad, Lichfield, 4d each.

Charges his feoffees (i.e. Marmyon, etc.) to allow Elizabeth to have possession of all the estates they hold during her lifetime, for the succour of her and their children. George, Earl of Shrewsbury and Sir John Savage, knight, to be supervisors of the will, Savage to have his young white gelding. The feoffees are to allow his executors, John Leek and Henry Marmyon (who are also feoffees) to occupy all his other lands in Derbyshire and Lincolnshire, and anywhere else in England, until his debts and legacies are paid and his children brought up. Each of his five daughters is to have 40 marks for their marriages, taken from the profits of his lands, and if more is available, the excess shall be divided between them, with the feoffees oversight. If Elizabeth is pregnant at this time, that child is to be raised and have the same 40 marks as the others.

If any die, their share is to be divided equally between the survivors. The daughters are to take the advice and counsel of his executors. Elizabeth is to have the hall with the demesne lands pertaining to it for 20 years, during her widowhood, paying the executors 14 marks per year, and she is to have custody of the children until they are 15 years old and to have 26s 8d for each of them from the executors. The executors are to receive all the profits of all the lands in feoffment in Derbyshire for 20 years, and of all the lands in Lincolnshire for 24 years. And, if the executors marry James Herdwyke, his son and heir, or if he comes to full age, then his marriage money shall be kept until he comes of age, and then delivered to James towards the setting up of his house.

Signed and sealed, with the proviso that the executors and feoffees shall not put out of their (illegible, presumably houses or lands) John Ekynfeld and John Turner, or take any fine, since they paid him two years before. Witnesses: Thomas Leek, gentleman; Sir Nicholas Strilley, vicar of Lownde; Sir Thomas Peeff, priest; Sir Robert Morton, priest; John Herdwyke of Maunsfeld, 'and many others.'

References and Notes

[1] S. M. Wright, *Derbyshire Gentry in the Fifteenth Century*, Derbyshire Record Society, 1983, 82

[2] The National Archive, hereafter TNA, E 150/743/8

[3] Ibid, 9-11

[4] TNA, E 150/743/8

[5] P. Riden, 'The Hardwicks of Hardwick Hall in the Fourteenth and Fifteenth Centuries', *Derbyshire Archaeological Journal* (hereafter, DAJ) vol 130, 2010, 148

[6] For a full discussion of the development of the Hardwick estate see P. Riden, and D. Fowkes, *Hardwick, a great house and its estate*, Phillimore, 2009, Chapter 2.

[7] See, for example, Folger Shakespeare Library, x. d. 428 (47 and 48)

8. B. J. Harris, *English Aristocratic Women, 1450¬1540*, OUP, 2002, 32-39. Lower gentry and 'gentlemen yeoman' looked to the social ranks above them for example and inspiration; E. Norton., *The Hidden Lives of Tudor Women*, Pegasus Books, 2018, 54-57

[9] Account Book of Sir William Cavendish and Lady Cavendish, 1548 to Michaelmas 1550, TNA, E 101/426/6: Folger, Shakespeare Library, x.d.486 (34). The accounts include payments of wages to "my sister Mary." D. N. Durant, *Bess of Hardwick: Portrait of an Elizabethan Dynast* Peter Owen Publishers (1999), 6-8, and 16, miss-identifies this woman as one of Ralph Leche's daughters by John Hardwick's widow. Harris, *op cit*, 262 n122 accepts Durant's identification. The entries in the account book clearly describe the Mary in question as being a 'Lady Cavendish' and must have been Sir William's stepsister Mary, the only child born to his father's second wife, Agnes. Mary remained unmarried and died at Chatsworth in 1556, the same year as Sir William and Bess's daughter, Mary, was born. It seems likely that baby Mary was named for her aunt.

[10] TNA, E 150/743/8

[11] T. Kilburn, 'Sir William Cavendish: Marriage to Bess and Relocation to Derbyshire', DAJ vol 139, 2019, 90; T. Kilburn, Hardwick Musing, 2021, 54

[12] Harris, op cit, 47

[13] See for example, Durant, Bess, 8 - 11: M. S. Lovell, *Bess of Hardwick: First Lady of Chatsworth*, Abacus, 2005, 19-20

[14] Folger x d 486 (14); Durant, Bess, 19

[15] Durant, Bess, 3: Lovell, Bess, 481: Riden, 'Hardwicks', 150-151: Kilburn, Musing, Chapter 5, part 1, 95-104

[16] Devonshire MSS, Chatsworth, Hardwick MSS, 7 Account Book of the Countess of Shrewsbury, 1591-97, fol. 195l.

[17] Riden, 'Hardwicks', 157: Kilburn, Musing, 120¬121

[18] Durant, Bess, 8: Lovell, Bess, 481

[19] A. Flower, *Tudor Women's Legal Rights, 1485¬1603*, 2007

[20] TNA, E 150/743/8

[21] Durant, Bess, 3

[22] Lovell, Bess, x, Hardwick family tree.

[23] Belvoir Castle Monuments, box labelled Pedigrees.

[24] TNA, C1/11/02/.32: Riden, 'Hardwicks', 151

[25] Derbyshire Local Studies Library, Local MS 6341, 18, cited by Riden, Hardwicks, 169

[26] Derbyshire Visitation Pedigrees, 1569 and 1611. 1895, London, 1895, 46; W. C. Metcalfe (ed,) *The Visitations of Derbyshire, 1569 and 1611*, Vol 7, 1891, 142)

[27] Derbyshire Local Studies Library, Local MS 6341, 18,

[28] British Library, Harleian Miscellany, 6592, 22, cited by Riden, Hardwicks, 169

[29] Belvoir Castle, op cit

[30] TNA, C1/651/13; Calendar of State Papers, Domestic. Edward VI, Mary, Elizabeth, and James I, Great Britain Public Records Office, 1856-1872. Thomas Seymour, Baron Seymour of Sudeley. Lord Seymour to the Duke of Somerset. 23 August 1548. MS Records Assembled by the State Paper Office SP 10/4 f.94.

[31] TNA, C1/860/14

[32] TNA, C1/860/15: Harris, op cit, 44

[33] Harris, *ibid*, 63. We know that Bess's uncle John Leake had connections with the Zouches of Codnor and that her sister Jane was in service with the Carews before her marriage to Godfrey Boswell. If Bess was ever in service to the Zouches, it would have to have been before her espousal to Robert Barley in 1536. However, there remains no definitive evidence that Bess was ever in service to the Zouches.

[34] TNA, STAC 2/7, FF. 15-16

[35] Riden, 'Hardwicks', 151, states that Robert Barley was born in January 1530.

[36] Flower, *Legal Rights, op cit,* 23

[37] Flower, *ibid*, 47: Harris, *op cit,* 61'-62; T. Stretton, *Women Waging War in Elizabethan England,* CUP, 1998, 21, 119, 129, 175. A femme sole was an unmarried woman and had few legal rights; a femme covert, was a married woman and she would be subject to the laws of coverture which included all her property becoming that of her husband. A widow was in a stronger position in that she was able to protect her property by use of pre-nuptial agreements.

[38] T. Kilburn, 'The Wardship and Marriage of Robert Barley, First Husband of Bess of Hardwick', DAJ, vol 134, 2014, 11-13, and Appendix 5; TNA c1/1101/17

[39] L. Stone, *Family, Sex and Marriage in England, 1500-1800*, Penguin, 1979, 30. Stone writes, "It cannot be emphasized too strongly that according to ecclesiastical law, the spousal was as legally binding a contract as the church wedding.". See also, D. Cressy, Birth, Marriage & Death: Ritual, Religion, and the Life-Cycle in Tudor and Stuart England, OUP, 1999, 316-332

[40] TNA, WARD 7/1/66 (no.164). Freschevile was clearly unaware of Robert's exact age.

[41] Cressy, *op cit*, 286; L. Stone, *The Crisis of the Aristocracy, 1558-1641*, OUP, 1979, 63-64; B. Coward, *Social Change and Continuity in Early Modern England, 1550-1750*, Longman, Studies in History, 1988, 20

[42] TNA, CP40/1120

[43] Kilburn, Musing, 14-15

[44] HMC, Cecil Papers, vol 16, 360.

[45] P. Riden, Sir William Cavendish: Tudor Civil Servant and Founder of a Dynasty, DAJ, vol 129, 2009, 254, n.108.

[46] Harris, op cit, 9-10, 39-40; Norton, op cit, 59

[47] TNA, C1/1102/37/39. 1545-46 appears to have been a critical period for John Hardwick's daughters encompassing as it is not only Boswell's case but also their brother James's coming out of wardship and entering fully into his inheritance; the death of John Leake; Bess's legal proceeding against George Barley and his guardian Peter Freschevile; and the commencement of her service most likely with Greys of Bradgate.

[48] TNA, STAC 2/17/53; TNA, STAC 2/22/359; TNA, STAC 2/22/40

[49] C.I. Merton, *The women who served Queen Mary and Queen Elizabeth: Ladies, Gentlewomen and Maids of the Privy Chamber, 1553 - 1603.* Unpublished PhD dissertation, Trinity College, Cambridge University, 1992, 263, 269

[50] Ibid, 48.

[51] See also https://folgerpedia.folger.edu/ Court: Women at Court; Royal Household. Sometimes misidentified as Bess is the sister of William St Loe, Elizabeth St Loe, who was among the first of Elizabeth I's Maids of Honour. Until the accession of Elizabeth I she had been in service to Elizabeth Stafford, Dowager Duchess of Norfolk, who died shortly after Elizabeth came to the throne.

[52] TNA C/78/78/14.

2. The Wardship and Marriage of Robert Barley, First Husband of Bess of Hardwick

In 2010, Philip Riden published an account of the Hardwick family of Hardwick Hall during the fifteenth and sixteenth centuries.[1] One of the questions he examined was the first of the four marriages of Elizabeth Hardwick, better known to history as 'Bess of Hardwick'.

Riden showed that much of the traditional account of how Bess met her first husband, Robert Barley, is at best fanciful. Although David Durant repeated the traditional account, he was the first to suggest that Robert's marriage to Bess was an arrangement made to mitigate the impact of wardship on the Barley estate.[2] Robert's father, Arthur Barley, had substantial debts even before he entered into his inheritance on the death of his father in 1533. A writ was issued against him in November 1530 for the sum of £100, which he owed to James Daniel, a London merchant taylor.[3] Marriage in the sixteenth century was often considered to be little more than a business transaction, a commodity to be bought and sold.

It is possible that his debts led Arthur to sell Robert's marriage and wardship in the 1530s rather than any pressing need to stave off the Court of Wards. Sometime between 1533 and 1538, Arthur sold Robert's wardship and marriage to Bess's stepfather, Ralph Leche. At a date no later than 1538, Ralph's debts led him to sell Robert's wardship and marriage to Henry Marmion. To avoid feudal dues and obligations, in June 1539 Arthur gifted his manors of Barley and Dunstone, together with all his properties in Derbyshire, to George Chaworth and Henry Marmion's brother-in-law, Gabriel Barwick. The lands were to be re-conveyed to Arthur for life before 24 August 1539 and thereafter were to pass to Robert and his heirs, then to Robert's brother George and his heirs and thereafter to any of Arthur's descendants.

The purpose of these feoffees to uses was to avoid being officially recognised in law as the legal holder. However, after Arthur's death, some of his lands were deemed to be held by knight service to the king. This led to Godfrey Boswell's purchase of Robert's wardship.[4] Robert was aged 13 when his father died on 28 May 1543. The exact date of Robert's marriage to Bess is not known though it is thought to have taken place in the spring of that year.[5] If so, it was destined to be of short duration as Robert died in December 1544.[6]

A chance discovery among recently digitised legal records at the National Archives has brought to light new evidence, which adds significantly to our understanding of Robert Barley's wardship and marriage.[7] It is an attachment responding to a plea submitted to the Court of Common Pleas during Hilary Term (Jan/Feb) 1544 by an attorney representing Peter Freschevile of Staveley. It requires the Derbyshire sheriff to attach certain persons who were to appear before the court on the quinidine of the following Easter Term (30 April 1544). At an unknown date in 1543, Freschevile had alleged that Ralph Leche, Elizabeth his wife, and Henry Marmion "…with force and arms they did take and abduct Robert Barley, having been found at Barley, the son and heir of Arthur Barley Esquire, being underage, whose marriage belongs to this Peter, against the will of this Peter."[8]

Bess's mother was first cousin to Peter Freschevile's mother, both women sharing the maiden name, Elizabeth Leake.[9] Ralph Leche married Bess's widowed mother in or about 1529.[10] The sheriff was also ordered to find Robert and place him in his safe keeping until the court determined to whom he was to be returned. Durant and others cite evidence from the Court of Wards to argue that Robert and Bess were married shortly before Arthur Barley's death on 28 May 1543. When Boswell acquired Robert's wardship it was stated that Robert was married in his father's lifetime.[11]

The Frescheviles claimed that the Barleys held the manor of Barlow by knight service of their manor of Staveley and that therefore they - the Frescheviles - held the rights of wardship and marriage should Barlow be inherited by an underage heir.[12] In June 1539 Arthur Barley made use of the Statute of Uses to free his Derbyshire manors and properties from feudal dues and obligations. The Barleys believed they held Barlow by socage and were therefore free to dispose of Robert's wardship and marriage as they chose. As far as the Frescheviles were concerned, Robert's wardship and marriage were not the Barleys to sell. Peter Freschevile has not previously been associated with Robert Barley's wardship and marriage, yet it is clear from his Common Pleas action that he considered himself to be Robert's lawful guardian and sought confirmation of this.

By 1538, Arthur Barley had sold Robert's wardship and marriage to Ralph Leche. In a Chancery bill dateable to no later than 1538, during a period in which Ralph was under pressure of debt, Henry Marmion stated that he had paid Ralph Leche £41 9s 2d for Robert's wardship and marriage.[13] In terms of common law, being of age meant being 21 or over. Freschevile stated that Robert was underage but did not comment on Bess's age. Robert was born in January 1530 and so in 1538 would have been about eight years of age.

When it came to marriage canon law held that boys were supposed to be at least 14 years of age. On the other hand, Bess, born in 1521 or 1522, would have been in her mid-teens and would have been considered 'of age' in terms of eligibility for marriage.[14] Marmion would have claimed still to hold Robert's wardship at the time of Robert's marriage to Bess, which probably explains why he was included in Freschevile's allegations of trespass and abduction.[15]

Although Robert's wardship and marriage appear to have been sold twice by 1538 it was not until 1543, shortly after Arthur Barley's death and Robert's marriage to Bess, that Freschevile commenced proceedings alleging that force had been used to abduct Robert. He claimed that Robert's marriage to Bess was illegal because he, as Robert's lawful guardian, had not consented to it. He clearly looked upon the marriage as a deliberate attempt to deprive him of his rights to Robert's wardship and with it control of the Barley inheritance during Robert's minority and perhaps longer. A marriage achieved by force was invalid and this is probably the reason Freschevile alleged that Robert had been abducted, and by implication, married under duress.[16]

After Robert's death, Freschevile became the lawful guardian of Robert's younger brother and heir, George Barley, who was thereafter married to Freschevile's daughter, Jane.[17] It is possible that Freschevile had intended Jane to marry Robert. If so, Bess's marriage to Robert threatened to thwart Freschevile's ambitions resulting in his taking action to uphold what he considered his legal rights as Robert's lawful guardian.

Plaintiffs and defendants almost habitually exaggerated the arguments that they or their attorneys put before the courts. Robert was taken to secure possession of his person. It is probable that to strengthen his case Freschevile exaggerated his claim that Robert had been abducted by force of arms. However, even allowing for a degree of exaggeration, Freschevile's allegations cannot be dismissed out of hand. Ralph Leche and Henry Marmion were variously accused in other legal actions in which the use of arms was alleged.

Among many dubious dealings, Ralph was accused of leading an assault on cattle in Mackworth. James Hardwick's guardian, John Bugby, was allegedly thrown out of Hardwick Hall by John Hardwick's executors, Henry Marmion and John Leake, in what was described as a violent assault on the property and in 1540/1 Marmion appears to have masterminded an alleged attack at Chatsworth for which he, Bess's mother and others, were brought before the Derby assizes and later investigated by Star Chamber.[18]

At the very least, Freschevile was challenging a marriage that had certainly taken place and his allegations demonstrate the lengths to which plaintiffs might go to support their cases in the courts. It remains unclear whether Freschevile was claiming that Robert had been kidnapped from an actual building, possibly the Barley's home at Barlow Lees which Ralph claimed to have purchased along with Robert's wardship, or whether the reference to Robert 'having been found at Barley' referred simply to the manor of Barlow. It is also unclear whether Freschevile's proceedings were solely concerned with the violation of what he took to be his rights as the Barley family's feudal overlord or whether they were rooted in a struggle for control not only of Robert's marriage but also his inheritance. Despite being encumbered with various debts and two claims for dower, this included land, timber, fishponds, coal, ironstone, smithies and bloomeries.[19]

Arthur Barley's widow, Elizabeth, sued for her dower but was unable to name Robert's guardian. Following Robert's death in December 1544 Freschevile became George Barley's guardian and in early 1545 promptly accepted her claim for dower without challenge.[20] It was at this time that in order to establish her legal rights to dower in the Barley estate Bess sued Freschevile and his ward George Barley in the Court of Common Pleas. However, Freschevile continued to maintain his belief that Bess's marriage to Robert had been illegal and he denied Bess's claim for dower. During 1545, two writs of dower were issued by the Court of Common Pleas to which after some prevarication Freschevile now claimed that Robert had never been seised of the estate from which Bess was seeking dower.

Bess answered that Freschevile's claim was false and intended simply to 'delay and fatigue' her dower proceeding. She stated that she had been without 'friends, aid or comfort', that her stepfather, Ralph Leche, then in the Fleet prison, stood 'condemned of great sums of money' and that neither she nor her mother could afford to continue to try the issue at Common Law. Early in 1546, Freschevile engaged Sir John Chaworth, Robert's uncle, to offer Bess an out-of-court settlement which she later argued was proof of her entitlement to dower. Freschevile offered to withdraw his claim and pay Bess dower providing she agreed to farm out her widow's third at an annual rent. Bess, 'enforced thereunto by necessity', accepted the advice of her counsel and agreed to these terms.

She estimated the value of her dower at £26 13s 4d (i.e. the 40 marks marriage portion left to her in her father's will). Chaworth offered only £16. Bess 'constrained by necessity than compelled by equity' reluctantly accepted Chaworth's offer, but at the eleventh hour, Freschevile reneged on the agreement determining instead to continue with his claim in the Court of Common Pleas. It was now, some eighteen months since Robert's death, that Bess turned to the equity courts and commenced proceedings against Freschevile and his ward George Barley in the Court of Chancery.

Bess's Common Pleas and Chancery actions were as much concerned with the legality of her marriage as they were about her dower. In her initial complaint to Chancery addressed to the Lord Chancellor, Sir Thomas Wriothesley, Bess explained how her marriage to Robert had come about. She was at pains to demonstrate that the marriage was lawful and, as had already been recorded in the Court of Wards, that it had taken place before the death of Robert's father. Bess informed Chancery that Arthur did 'covenant and bargain' and had been paid 'diverse great sums of money' for her marriage to Robert. It has been assumed that these events took place in 1543 but Bess did not state when they had taken place. Her sole reference to the year 1543 was in relation to Robert's inheritance on the death of his father. It seems probable that Ralph Leche had in mind a marriage with Bess when he first purchased Robert's wardship and marriage from Arthur Barley some years before 1543 and that this remained the intention when Ralph sold Robert's wardship and marriage to Henry Marmion. It is reasonable to assume that Arthur had been paid for Robert's wardship and marriage when Ralph Leche had purchased them and that 'being then but of tender years' Robert and Bess were espoused at that time but Robert was too young to consummate the marriage. [21]

Bess informed Chancery that various payments had been made to Arthur Barley, but it is unclear who had made them.[22] She may have been referring to the monies paid for Robert's wardship and marriage by Ralph and Henry

Marmion. Riden has demonstrated the precarious nature of Ralph's finances.[23] In 1537 Ralph was sued for debt in the Court of Common Pleas by Sir John Byron. Byron sued again the following year when Ralph was amongst the defendants who were facing proceedings for debt commenced by Henry Bird, a Yeoman of the Chamber.[24]

In 1538, Bess's mother accused Ralph of desertion and leaving her and the children Ralph had fathered by her on the verge of destitution, dependent on the charity of friends and neighbours.[25] An undated Star Chamber account refers to legal process in the London Guildhall regarding the administration of a case before the mayoral court between July and October 1538 brought by Ralph against Arthur Barley relating to the recovery of a debt of 100 marks. The nature of the debt is not given but Arthur lost the case and was imprisoned in London's Poultry Compter. The writ by which he was imprisoned, dated the 4th of July 1538, stated that he should remain in prison until he had paid Ralph the 100 marks plus £3 damages. However, on 17 July, William Pickering, an attorney acting on behalf of Ralph Aleyn, alleged that Ralph owed Aleyn a debt of £103.

Aleyn claimed that on the 1st of April 1534, in the parish of St Christopher in Cheap ward, London, by a bill of obligation sealed with his seal and presented to the court, Leche acknowledged that he owed Aleyn £200, payable at Pentecost in the following year—24th May 1535—but thus far Ralph had only paid £97 and had refused several requests to pay the balance of £103. Summonses were issued requiring Ralph to appear before the mayoral court to answer Aleyn's plea but he failed to do so. On 6 October 1538, in accordance with the custom of the city of London, it was ordered that the £69 3 s 4d owed to Ralph by Arthur Barley should be paid to Ralph Aleyn as partial repayment of the outstanding £103 owed to him thus leaving Leche to find the remaining balance of £30 6s 8d of his debt to Aleyn.[26] Bess herself referred to Ralph's heavy debts in her dower proceedings and he was to spend time in the Fleet prison in 1538 and again in the mid-1540s, the latter partly in consequence of a long-running dispute with Henry Sacheverell and Dame Elizabeth Savage which included accusations of debt, theft and forgery.[27]

Perhaps aware of his own nearness to death and the need to minimise the impact that wardship would have on his family and estates, Arthur Barley eventually sought to complete Robert's marriage. Bess did not inform Chancery of the date of her marriage to Robert although her initial complaint to the court clearly indicates that it took place before Arthur Barley's death. There is no evidence that Robert and Bess ever lived together as man and wife. However, it was common for the espoused female to join the household of the person to whom she was espoused.

Ralph Leche does not appear to have been willing to maintain John Hardwick's daughters beyond the age of 15 years. When John and Anne Wykes visited Hardwick in the summer of 1540, of John Hardwick's surviving four daughters, only Jane and Mary appear to have been in residence at the family home. It remains possible that Bess was then living with the Barleys and may have been from the time of the espousal contact of 1536.

Robert was just short of his fifteenth birthday when he died in December 1544. The main beneficiary of his death was undoubtedly Peter Freschevile as it ensured there would be no heir from the marriage to Bess. As the guardian of Robert's heir George Barley, Freschevile gained what he had wanted. His interest in Robert's wardship ended with Robert's death but, having lost the Barley wardship once, Freschevile was determined not to lose it a second time. There was to be no challenge to his wardship of George Barley which he claimed as 'lord of the fee', the basis on which he had previously asserted his rights to Robert's wardship.[28] Robert's death would also have brought an end to Freschevile's legal proceedings against Robert's marriage to Bess and also led to her attempts to secure her widow's dower.

In early February 1548, a recognisance was agreed in King's Bench in which Freschevile was to permit Bess to enter fully into her Barley dower until George Barley reached the age of majority or until such time as Freschevile could prove that Sir William and Bess were not legally entitled to dower.[29] Freschevile was to pay dower arrears of £60 7s to Sir William and Bess, or to either one of them, in two instalments of £30 3 s 6d to be paid on the Feast of the Nativity of St John the Baptist(24th of June) and the Feast of All Saints (1st of November). Both payments were to be made 'att the mansyon howse of James Hardwyke Esquier callid Hardwike Hall'.

Bess was five months pregnant when this agreement was reached. She was with Sir William at his Northaw home in late May 1548 when the Northaw enclosure riots took place and their first child, Frances, was born at Northaw on the 18th of June 1548. It is unlikely that Bess or her husband would have been at Hardwick to receive Freschevile's first instalment on 24th June. However, once secured Bess received her Barley dower for the remainder of her life.

The chance discovery of part of Peter Freschevile's 1543/4 Court of Common Pleas proceedings against Ralph Leche, Elizabeth his wife, and Henry Marmion, sheds new light on the wardship and marriage of Robert Barley. Freschevile's allegations of trespass and the forcible abduction of Robert Barley may have been no more than legal fiction since he certainly had ample motive to lie to the courts, but his previously unknown involvement in Robert's wardship and marriage adds a new dimension to the narrative. For the first time, we can place Peter Freschevile at the centre of the events and in consequence offer a revised interpretation of Robert's marriage to Bess of Hardwick.

Chapter 2: Appendices

APPENDIX 1: Peter Freschevile's allegations of the abduction and illegal marriage of Robert Barley, TNA, CP 40/1120 (AALT IMG 7469), Hilary Term, 1544. The National Archive CP 40/1120

Crown copyright

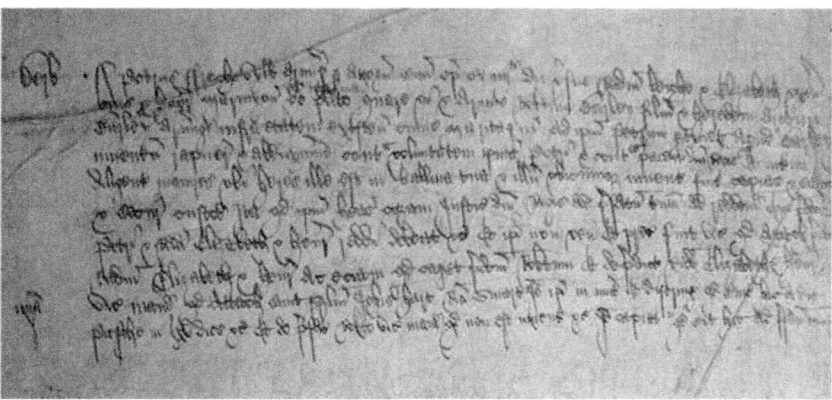

Derbyshire

Peter Frechevyll Esquire by his attorney brought a case on the fourth day against Ralph Leiche and Elizabeth his wife and Henry Marmyon \of … man/ concerning a plea why with force and arms they did take and abduct Robert Barley, having been found at Barley, the son and heir of Arthur Barley Esquire, being underage, whose marriage belongs to this Peter, against the will of this Peter and against the peace of the Lord the King, And meanwhile you shall diligently enquire where he the heir is in your bailiwick, and wheresoever you shall find him you shall take him and keep him safely and securely so that you shall have him before the Justices of the Lord the King at the said term to return unto whom of the said Peter and Ralph Elizabeth and Henry he ought to return etc. And they did not come. The Sheriff was ordered to attach Ralph Elizabeth and Henry and also that he should seize the said Robert. And concerning the said Ralph Elizabeth and Henry the Sheriff orders that they are attached by the pledge of John Hart and Richard Smart. Therefore, they are in mercy. And distrain them so that they be here on the Quinidine of Easter[*] etc. And concerning the said Robert the Sheriff orders that he is not found etc., so he should be seized so that he be here at the said term.

* 15 April 1544

APPENDIX 2: Godfrey Boswell's purchase of Robert Barley's wardship, 1544. The National Archive, WARD 9/152.Crown copyright.

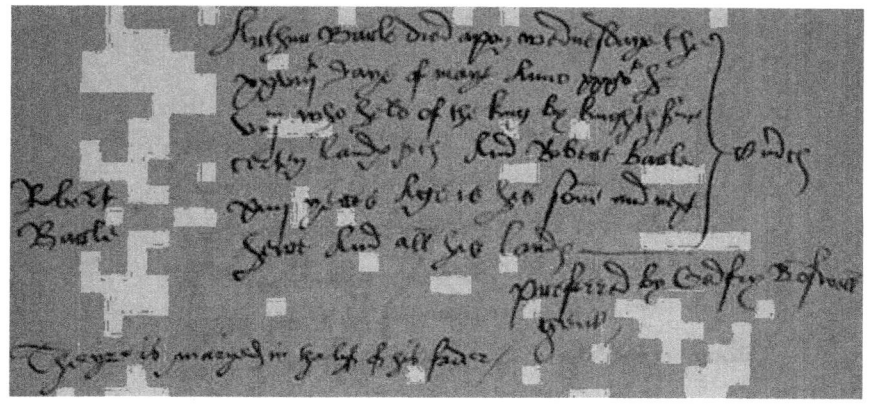

	Arthur Barle died upon Wednesday	
Robert Barle	the xxviijth day of may Anno xxxvth	
	[35] H[enry] Viij who held of the king	100
	by knight s[er]vice certain lands etc	marks
	And Robert xiiii years Age is his son	
	and next heir And all his	

lands preferred by Godfry Boswell/gent /

The heir is married in the life of his father /

51

APPENDIX 3: Transcript of, Bess of Hardwick's complaint to Chancery, Trinity Term (20 June to mid-July), 1546. TNA, C 1/1101/17.

To the right honourable Sir Thomas Wryothesley, knight of the honourable order of the garter, Lord Wryothesley and Lord Chancellor of England.

In most humble wise complaining showeth unto your honourable lordship your daily oratrice Elizabeth Barley, widow, late the wife of Robert Barley, esquire, deceased, son and heir of//

Arthur Barley, esquire, also deceased, that whereas the said Arthur Barley was lawfully seised of and in the manor of Barley with appurtenances in the county of Derby, and of [...]// messuages, ten cottages, one thousand acres of land, three hundred acres of meadow, six hundred acres of pasture, four hundred acres of wood, six hundred acres of furze and heath, and// ten pounds of rent with their appurtenances in Barlow, Barlow Lees, Dunston, Dronfield and Holmesfield in the said county of Derby, in his demesne as of fee, all which manor, lands, tenements and// premises being of the yearly value of £80 and above, and the said Arthur Barley, so being seised of the said manor, lands, tenements and premises, did covenant and bargain with the friends// of your said oratrice for a marriage to be had between the said Robert and your said oratrice, in consideration of diverse great sums of money paid by the friends of the same your// oratrice to the said Arthur for the same, in the performance of which said bargain the said Robert Barley was lawfully married and espoused unto your said oratrice, the same Robert and// your said oratrice being then but of tender years. And after, the said Arthur, so as is aforesaid being seised of the said manors, lands, tenements and premises in his demesne as of fee [...]// such estate thereof seised in the 35th year [22 April 1543 to 22 April 1544] of the reign of our sovereign lord the king that now is, the said Robert being then of the age of 13 years, after whose decease the said manor,// lands, tenements and premises descended unto the said Robert Barley, as son and heir of the said Arthur, by force whereof the same Robert was lawfully seised of and in the said manor,// lands, tenements and all other the premises in his demesne as of fee. And the said Robert, so being seised of the premises, about the last day of December in the 36th year [22 April 1544 to 22 April 1545] of the// reign of our sovereign lord the king that now is [Henry VIII] of such estate thereof died seised without any issue of his body lawfully begotten, after whose decease the said manor, lands, [...]// premises being descended unto George Barley, esquire, as brother and heir

52

of the said Robert, the same George being within the age of 21 years, by reason whereof Sir Peter// Frechevyle, knight, supposing the said manor of Barley, parcel of the premises, to be holden of him by knight service, hath entered into the same manor of Barley [with appurtenances?]// and hath the custody of the body of the same George and the residue of all the said lands, tenements and premises being in the hands of the said George, by reason that [...] are// holden in socage, and that the same George is of the age of 14 years and [...] after the decease of which said Robert Barley for that your said oratrice is by the [...]// usual laws of this realm lawfully entitled to be endowed of the third part of the said manor, lands, tenements and all other the premises she demanded and [...]// the said Sir Peter as the said George to assign unto her the said dower thereof, which they unjustly and against all laws and equity refused to do, whereupon [...]// oratrice was compelled to sue against the said Sir Peter and George Barley two several writs of dower returnable before the justices of our sovereign lord the [...]// his common place at Westminster, to be endowed of the third part of premises, in the which said writs, after the same had long depended before the said [...]// any answer made unto the same, to the great cost and charge and delay of your said poor oratrice, the said Sir Peter and the said George by the procurement [?of the]// same Sir Peter, untruly pleaded that the said Robert Barley, during the espousal and marriage between him and your said oratrice, was never seised [...]// estate whereof she ought to be endowed, which said plea is untrue and only pleaded to the intent to delay and fatigue your said poor oratrice, being [...]// friends, aid or comfort and not able to try the said issue untruly tendered by the said Sir Peter and George by the order of the common laws [...]// thereby to accept a final recompense for her said lawful dower at the pleasure of the said Sir Peter and George, for since the said untrue plea pleaded [...]// to say in the term of Saint Hilary [20 January to mid-February]—in the 37th year [April 1545 to April 1546] of the reign of our said sovereign lord, Sir John Chaworth, knight, uncle to the said George, by his [...]// and assent of the said Sir Peter as of the said George, knowing right well that your said oratrice ought to be endowed of the premises and diverse [...]// proffer unto the council of your said oratrice that if she would be contented to demise and let to farm all her said third part of the premises [...]// friends for a certain yearly rent to be reserved for the same, that then they would waive and relinquish the said untrue plea and issue and [...]// poor oratrice, which thing your said oratrice, being enforced thereunto by necessity, by the advice of her council, was contented to do, and [...]// the said Sir John Chaworth and the council of your said oratrice, the same Sir John Chaworth would not assent that there should [...]// upon the said demised and fortreated lease of the said third part, but only £16, where of truth the just third part of the same [...]// £26 13s 4d, which notwithstanding your said oratrice rather constrained by necessity than compelled by equity, was contented to accept [...]// her dower, which the said Sir John Chaworth also refused, by reason whereof the said untrue plea remaining now to be tried [...]// the king's justices of nisi prius, wherein the said Sir Peter and George are inhabiting, and your said poor oratrice without any friends [...]// her to her trial of her said just title. And so, right honourable lord, for as much as Ralph Leeche, who hath married the mother of your said [...]// condemned in great sums of money and her said mother very poor and not able to relieve herself and much less your said oratrice, and for [...]// not nor had any substance or other advancement but only the said title of dower by her said late husband who died, being very ly[...]// not of ability to proceed to the trial of the said issues and untrue pleas against the said Sir Peter and George by the order of the common law [...]// for the same, suffering the said most apparent wrong and injuries, living as she hath done by the space of one year and a half since the [...]// succour or comfort of the said lands. In tender consideration whereof it may please your good lordship to grant the king's gracious w[rit?] [...]// Sir Peter and George straightly enjoining and commanding them by the same upon a certain pain by your good lordship[...]// oratrice her lawful third part of the said manor, lands, tenements and premises, and to pay unto her all the arrears [...]// the decease of her said late husband, or else to permit and suffer the same your oratrice to have, occupy and enjoy the third part [...]// premises and the rents and revenues of the same third part, to have and take to her own proper use, without any impediment [...]// Frechevyle and George or any of them, or of any person or persons by their commandment, procurement or consent, or to their use [...]// otherwise licensed by your good lordship, and your said poor oratrice shall daily pray to God for the good estate of your good lor[dship] [...]//

References and Notes

[1] P. Riden. 'The Hardwicks of Hardwick Hall in the Fifteenth and Sixteenth Centuries', *Derbyshire Archaeological Journal*, 130 (2010), 142 - 75. I am grateful to Philip Riden and Maureen Taylor for their helpful comments during the writing of this article.

[2] D. Durant, *Bess of Hardwick: Portrait of an Elizabethan Dynast* (1999), 8-11. The assertion that Bess had been in service to the Zouches of Codnor comes from Nathaniel Johnson who in 1692 claimed he had been told by some "ancient gentlemen" that Bess met Robert Barley when she was in service to an otherwise unidentified "Lady Zouche" in London where Robert, also in service to Johnson's Lady Zouche, was lying sick. There were two Lady Zouches residents at Codnor at that time, Lady Margaret Zouche and her daughter-in-law, Lady Anne Zouche. In fact, there is not a single shred of contemporary evidence to indicate that Bess or Robert were ever in service to the Zouches and neither Bess nor Robert Barley were in London when their marriage took place. Johnson also repeated Sir William Dugdale's claim that Robert had left Bess all his lands and thereby she became a wealthy widow, W. Dugdale, *Baronage of England,* 1675, ii, 420¬2. This also has no historical foundation. Robert's estate was inherited by his brother, George. Given that Robert's mother and grandmother were also entitled to dower from the estate, Bess could only claim one-third of a widow's third (i.e., 1/9th), Riden, 'The Hardwicks', 152, 169. Bess herself estimated her dower entitlement as £26 13s 4d whereas Sir John Chaworth, acting as arbiter, valued it at £16. Suffice it to say that Bess certainly did not become a wealthy widow on Robert's death. Writing well over a century and more after the events both Johnson and Dugdale faced an almost complete lack of evidence of Bess's early years. Confronted with the need to explain how a woman of relatively modest birth became a wealthy countess, between them. Dugdale and Johnson produced a plausible story which, not surprisingly, went unchallenged at the time and came to be rehashed as fact in the writings of later authors.

[3] The National Archives (TNA), C 241/282/103.

[4] Henry Marmion and John Leake were the executors of the will of Bess's father, John Hardwick. TNA C 1/860/14-15 cited by Riden, 'The Hardwicks', 151-3 and n. 72, 169, is a Chancery case commenced at some point between 1533 and 1538 by Henry Marmion against Ralph Leche, Richard Penniston and William Curtenhall. Marmion claimed the

rent of Lees Hall which had been sold with the wardship and marriage of Robert, son and heir apparent of Arthur Barley. TNA C 1/860/14-15 states that 'Arthur Barley, esquire, sold the wardship and marriage of one Robert Barley, his son and heir apparent, to one Rauf Leyche, esquire' (that bit is interlined, but perfectly clear), and then enfeoffed certain lands in Derbyshire worth £10 4d to others, to the use of Ralph who in great debt then sold the marriage, wardship and keeping of the lands to Marmion for £41 9s 2d'. These proceedings took place during the chancellorship of Thomas Audley who was Lord Chancellor between 1532 and 1544 but after his elevation in 1538 would have been addressed as Baron or Lord Audley. Interestingly, in a document dated 5 June 1539, Arthur Barley gifted all his lands in Derbyshire to George Chaworth and Henry Marmion's brother-in-law and close associate, Gabriel Barwick. As feoffees Chaworth and Barwick were to re-convey the lands back to Arthur Barley before 24 August. Nottinghamshire Archives, DD/P/CD/113. This feoffment to use was the usual device landowners executed towards the end of their lives so that their heir could show the escheator that the deceased had held nothing in chief at the time of his death. Thus, around the same time as Marmion claimed he had purchased Robert's wardship and marriage from Ralph Leche, Arthur Barley was clearly attempting to free his lands of feudal dues and obligations. On Boswell, aka Bosvile, see Durant, Bess, 10, where he states that at some point after Arthur Barley's death, and before the death of Robert, Robert's wardship was sold for 100 marks to Bess's brother-in-law, Godfrey Boswell, but Durant does not say from whom Boswell made the purchase. It was, in fact, purchased from the crown. TNA, WARD 7/1/66 (no.164), following Arthur Barley's death Chancery issued a writ for an Inquisition Post-Mortem held at Bolsover on the 12th of October 1543. Among other items, the jurors found Arthur held his lands at Barley Lees by knight service to the king—which superseded Freschevile's claim—and had left an heir within age. In the case of inheritance being 'within age' meant under 21. Chancery would have been informed and alerted the Court of Wards. TNA, WARD 9/152 spans the period 22 April 1539 to 21 April 1546. The Court of Wards record of the sale of his wardship states that Robert was fourteen years old. He was born in January 1530 and therefore Boswell must have made the purchase in 1544. See Appendix 2. Boswell entered into his inheritance on the death of his father in 1542. He married Bess's sister, Jane [aka Joan] who is described as Boswell's wife in a Court of Common Pleas case begun in 1545/6 by Sir James Foljambe. TNA, CP40/1124 (AALT IMG f346 and IMG f924). See Ch 6 for more on Boswell's purchase of Robert's wardship.

[5] Riden, 'The Hardwicks', 151-2 and nn 72-3, citing TNA, C 142/282/103. There were three stages to marriage in the sixteenth century: espousal, marriage ceremony, and consummation. Although considered married on espousal there could be many years between the espousal and the marriage ceremony.

[6] Riden, 'The Hardwicks', 169. Under Canon Law, a marriage between a boy over the age of 14 and a girl over the age of 12 could not be dissolved because it could be

consummated. Child marriages, on the other hand, could be and often were dissolved. Thirteen years old in January 1543, Robert was under the age of 14 when his marriage to Bess took place and, therefore, potentially under Canon Law, the marriage could have been dissolved.

[7] Over eight million images from several classes of medieval and early modern legal records at the National Archives have been digitized by the University of Houston's O'Quinn Law Library. The Anglo-American Legal Tradition digital archive assembled by Robert C. Palmer, Elspeth K. Palmer and Susanne Jenks is available at http://aalt.law.uh.edu/aalt.html (AALT)

[8] TNA, CP 40/1120 (AALT IMG 7469); see Appendix 1. I am grateful to Peter Foden for the translation of the original Latin text of Appendix 1. The document (Appendix 1) dates from late February-March 1544 and this suggests that Freschevile had most likely lodged his plea in the Court of Common Pleas in the spring of 1543. The proceedings appear to have dragged on over many months and may never have reached a conclusion. Ralph Leche, Bess's mother Elizabeth, and Henry Marmion were to appear before the court together with Robert Barley on the quindene of the Easter term, 1544, 30 April. Ralph Leche would have moved swiftly to secure Robert's marriage to Bess within as short a time as possible, any delay would have been advantageous to Freschevile. If Robert and Bess were married shortly before Arthur Barley's death on 28 May 1543 Freschevile could be expected to have raised his objections at that time.

[9] Peter Freschevile's mother was the daughter of John Leake and Elizabeth Savage. Bess's mother was the daughter of Thomas Leake and Margaret Fox. John and Thomas were the sons of William Leake of Sutton and Katherine Chaworth. 'Pedigree of the Freschevile and Musard Families', *Collectanea Topographica et Genealogica*, 4 (1837), 4; In a box labelled 'pedigrees' in Belvoir Castle Muniments is a book of manuscript pedigrees of landed families c.1565. The unknown genealogist was trying to explain contemporary allegiances. Among the hand-drawn pedigrees is one titled 'Leeke Grey and Frechvyle' which includes the marriage of Elizabeth Leake to John Freschevile.

[10] Riden, 'The Hardwicks', 153.

[11] TNA, WARD 9/152, see Appendix 2. Although there is no suggestion that Robert had married anyone else, this document doesn't say who Robert married. The statement that Robert had married before the death of his father is commonly cited as evidence that Robert and Bess were married prior to Arthur Barley's death. However, such a statement had special relevance in cases of wardship because the impact of wardship was greater in cases where an under-age heir was unmarried. The statement that Robert had married in the lifetime of his father may have been added simply to reduce the impact of wardship and on its own may not be reliable evidence of the date of Robert's marriage to Bess. When he reached the age of maturity in 1553 George Barley sued Freschevile, Sir William Cavendish, Bess, and Edward Bowne, an attorney in the Common Bench, for spoiling his estates. TNA, C 1/1291/17 (dateable to the first half of 1553). Among the

replies of the defendants is one made by Sir William and Bess which states that Robert was already seised of his estates when he married Bess, TNA, C 1/1291/17. This would imply that Robert's marriage to Bess had taken place shortly after Arthur Barley's death.
[12] Riden, 'The Hardwicks', 152. TNA, C 1/1291/17-21. From the early fourteenth century, the Barleys are recorded as holding lands and tenements in Barley partly by half a knight's service of the Freschevile's manor of Staveley. Collectanea, 183. Arthur Barley's IPM states that the manor of Barley was held of Peter Frechewell, esquire, as of two parts of his manor of Staveley, by service of half a knight's fee and suit of court, and worth £13 6s 8d p.a', TNA, WARD 7/1/66 (no.164), E 150/753/2 and C 142/68/51. George Barley continued to seek redress and in 1559, following the death of Freschevile in 1558, he petitioned Lord Keeper Bacon stating in his submission that 'After Robert died, Sir Peter Frechevyle, now deceased, a man then of great power, without right entered the lands, claiming to be George's guardian, supposing the lands to be held of him by knight service, when in fact they are held by socage tenure and not by knight service'. George claimed he had no remedy at common law against the administrator for the deeds of Sir Peter, and thus asked for a writ of subpoena to Sir Peter's heir, Peter Freschevile, esquire, ordering him to appear in Chancery, to answer the charges and abide by the court's decision. TNA, C 3/11/108.
[13] Riden, 'The Hardwicks', n. 72, 169, citing TNA, C 1/860/14-15. This was also the period during which Ralph was facing imprisonment in the Fleet and accusations of desertion by his wife. Nottinghamshire Archives, DD/P/CD/113.
[14] TNA, C1/1101/17; T. Kilburn, 'Wardship and Marriage of Robert Barley, First Husband of Bess of Hardwick' Derbyshire Archaeological Journal, Vol 134, 2014. Riden, 'The Hardwicks of Hardwick Hall in the Fifteenth and Sixteenth Centuries', Derbyshire Archaeological Journal, 130 (2010), 151.
[15] In his will John Hardwick appointed Henry Marmion and John Leake as guardians of his children, a guardianship which would have ceased when his son came of age and when each of his daughters married or in terms of Common Law came of age.
[16] Flower, Tudor Women's Legal Rights, 1485-1603 (2007), 25
[17] G. D. Barlow, Published Matter and Records relating to the Families of the Name Barlow (1911), contains a printed pedigree based on the visitations of 1569 and 1611 inserted after page 20. Sir Montague Barlow, Barlow Family Records (1932). Pedigree number 5, inserted between pages 16 - 17. The Belvoir Castle manuscript pedigree, see n.9 above, includes the marriage of George Barley to Jane Freschevile.
[18] The case against Ralph was brought by Robert Stokes, TNA: STAC 2/28/49; Riden., 'The Hardwicks', 157; Wykes v Waterhouse, TNA: STAC: 20/2/40, fol 1r.
[19] Riden, ibid, 151-2
[20] In 1543 Robert's mother, Elizabeth Barley, Arthur Barley's widow, began a Common Pleas action for dower, Hilary Term, 1544, against Robert Barley, Peter Freschevile esq, Ralph Leche and Henry Marmion. TNA, CP 40/1120 (AALT IMG 5387). Her case was

contemporaneous with Freschevile's proceedings against Ralph Leche, Bess's mother, and Marmion. Although her son Robert was still a minor, she was unable to identify his guardian, presumably because the court was yet to determine Freschevile's case. Her claim for dower was accepted unchallenged by Freschevile, Easter Term, 1545. TNA, CP 40/1125 (AALT IMG 0262). Bess's cousin, Catherine Leake, married Sir Godfrey Foljambe. Their son, Sir George, married Robert's sister, Dorothy. The Foljambes were also suing Freschevile for Dorothy's unpaid marriage portion.

[21] TNA, C 1/1101/17, Appendix 3, is Bess's initial complaint to Chancery presented to Sir Thomas Wriothesley who became Lord Chancellor on the 3rd of May 1544. Bess informed Chancery that she had been a widow for eighteen months which indicates that she began her Chancery action in mid-1546. The final section of the document is irreparably damaged with many words missing but provides details of Bess's attempts to obtain dower including references to her 1545 Common Pleas proceedings and to events that had taken place earlier in 1546. Bess also refers to having been "married and espoused" to Robert but later reverses the order to "espoused and married". Wright, Derbyshire Gentry, 122, argues it was common practice among the gentry of north-east Derbyshire to engage an arbiter to resolve disputes even when court proceedings were already in progress. The Chaworths were related to the Frescheviles, the Leakes, the Hardwicks and the Barleys, and had acted as feofees of certain Hardwick and Barley lands. TNA, WARD 7/1/66 (no.164).

[22] TNA, C 1/1101/17 states that Arthur Barley was paid by the '[…]' of Elizabeth. Unfortunately, the word here is faded and virtually illegible, even under UV light, although it is almost certainly one word and given the context in which it occurs is most likely the word 'friends' by which Bess may have meant Ralph Leche and Henry Marmion and possibly Godfrey Boswell.

[23] For a detailed discussion of Ralph's finances see Riden, 'The Hardwicks', 153-5.

[24] TNA, CP 40/1092 (AALT IMG 2706); TNA, CP 40/1096 (AALT IMG 2393)

[25] Riden, 'The Hardwicks', 155. As husband and wife were considered a 'single soul', Bess's mother could not sue Ralph under Common Law but could do so in a court of equity. TNA, C1 845/34. Flower, *Legal Rights*, 15. Frechevile's proceedings suggest that Ralph and Elizabeth were reconciled no later than 1543.

[26] TNA, STAC 2/19/310 Ralph's plea for debt against Arthur Barley and Ralph Aleyn's case against Leche. The Poultry Compter, in the parish of St Mildred, Cheap ward, was one of several debtors' prisons under the control of the city of London sheriffs.

[27] Riden, 'The Hardwicks', 153-4

[28] TNA, C 1/1101/17.

[29] TNA, CP40/1135.

3. Sir William Cavendish: Marriage to Bess and Relocation to Derbyshire

Four times the nuptial bed she warm'd,
And every time so well perform'd,
That when death spoil'd,
each husband's billing,
He left the widow every shilling...

– Walpole

Horace Walpole was not impressed with Hardwick Hall. It was not to his taste. Having been told he would be utterly charmed by the house, he wrote, 'Never was I less charmed in my life'. Referring to Bess as 'that old beldam', he determined to write her an 'epitaph'.[1]

Walpole was not the first, nor would he be the last, to portray Bess as a consummate schemer. In 1672, Sir William Dugdale wrote that Bess 'became Mistriss of a very vast fortune, by her successful matching with several wealthy Husbands'.[2] In 1838 Edmund Lodge stated that Bess, "unsated with the wealth and the caresses of three husbands finished her conquests by marrying the Earl of Shrewsbury, the richest and most powerful peer of his time."[3] These authors failed to recognise that Bess had to struggle through both common law and equity courts to secure dower from her marriage to Robert Barley[4] and she was said to be penniless when Sir William Cavendish died in 1557.[5]

Despite two previous marriages, Cavendish was still in need of a male heir at the time of his marriage to Bess. Shortly after the marriage, he commenced his move to Derbyshire. Philip Riden has noted that both Sir William's marriage to Bess and his subsequent decision to relocate lock, stock and barrel to Derbyshire have 'never been satisfactorily explained'.[6] The first to claim that Sir William's move to Chatsworth came at the 'desire' of Bess was Arthur Collins in 1752, though without explaining what that desire was.[7]

It has been suggested that the only reason to accept Collins's statement is that 'it is difficult to think of any other reason why an official at court would give up an estate conveniently close to London... and move to a much more remote county...'.[8] Cavendish was not alone among his rank and calling to seek to create a land-based posterity but was the choice of Derbyshire merely to satisfy the whim of his new wife, as some have supposed?

Sir William Cavendish
© National Trust Images

In May 1548, Sir William's principal estate at Northaw, Hertfordshire, became the target of anti-enclosure riots. Local protests over Cavendish's use of common land erupted in 1544 when he attempted to enclose some 500 acres of Northaw Great Waste.[9] He was alleged to have over-stocked the commons with rabbits and sheep. The 1548 riots were a continuation of this dispute, a reaction to a royal commission granted to Sir William in the king's name by the newly appointed Lord Protector, Edward Seymour. Cavendish claimed that on May 21 around sixty rioters camped outside his house and laid siege to the property. Sir William, a heavily pregnant Bess, other members of his family and visitors to the property were trapped inside.

Cavendish alleged that numerous attempts were made to break into the house and that the rioters threatened to burn down the property and all those within if he did not come out and face them. They inflicted considerable damage at Northaw, including the use of explosives to destroy Sir William's rabbit warrens along with around 1,000 rabbits on Northaw Common. A second attack on the warrens took place the following day, May 22, resulting in the deaths of a further 300 rabbits slaughtered 'amidst a volley of bone-chilling cries'. Cavendish alleged that his chaplain and some of his servants were attacked during the rioting.

On the nights of 25 and 26 May, Sir William claimed to have been awakened by 'hallowing, cryeng and yelling' coming from outside his house, frightening his wife and family, as the rioters continued to hunt in the nearby warrens, and that during the first night the rioters stole a trotting horse and five geldings from his stables.[10] We cannot rule out the possibility that these events caused great distress to Bess and led her to wish to return to her roots but does this factor alone explain Sir William's decision move to Derbyshire?

The rioting at Northaw was over by 1548. The well-known anti-enclosure movement of 1549 was suppressed during the late summer and early autumn of that year. Cavendish's purchase of Chatsworth and Cromford did not take place until December 1549, some eighteen months after the Northaw riots and his relocation to Derbyshire was not completed until 1552.[11]

The rioting at Northaw, which had begun in 1544, simmered on until 1548. It reflected local grievances borne by the tenants against the activities of a relative newcomer and presaged the widespread anti-enclosure movement of 1549. It has been suggested that Sir William 'may have been driven out of Hertfordshire by local animosity'[12] though he was still being described as of Northaw, Chatsworth and London in 1553.[13] The 1549 anti-enclosure disturbances did, however, play a significant role in the demise of Protector Somerset.

In seeking to explain both Sir William's marriage to Bess and his relocation to Derbyshire historians may have been looking in the wrong place. Could Sir William's decisions have been influenced far more by events at the centre of government during and after Edward VI's reign than has been recognised? Can it be a mere chance that his move to Derbyshire coincided with Edward Seymour's fall from power and the later attempt to place Lady Jane Grey on the throne? Are there too many such 'coincidences' for them to be ignored? Those familiar with the high politics of the mid-sixteenth century, a period often referred to as the mid-Tudor crisis,[14] will recognise the difficulties in acquiring a full understanding of affairs at court, the epicentre of political life during this tumultuous period.

The politics of the period remain steeped in obfuscation as over the intervening centuries untruths have been told and documents distorted, destroyed or otherwise 'lost', whilst many of those involved sought to cover up their roles in the dramas that afflicted the realm at this critical juncture in English history. The simplest way to prove guilt was to use the words of the accused against them. A search of an accused person's private papers would be among the first stages of any investigation and those accused would look to destroy such evidence before it could be found.

The last word often written at the end of letters containing incriminating material was 'burn'. As John Flower put it to Thomas Seymour in 1548, once gone such evidence 'shall tell no more tales.'[15] Much of Thomas Cromwell's correspondence disappeared. Shortly before his arrest in October 1549 Thomas Seymour's brother, Edward Seymour, Lord Protector, gave orders that his papers should be destroyed. Mary, Queen of Scots, instructed Anthony Babington to burn her ciphered letters and following his abortive revolt in 1601 the Earl of Essex busied himself setting fire to his papers.[16] Bess also learned this lesson. In a letter of c1570, she told her husband, George Talbot, to burn a letter she had written to him which contained sensitive material.[17]

Bess's first marriage to Robert Barley lasted less than two years. The notion that Bess became a wealthy woman on Robert's death is false. The family estate was inherited, not by Bess, but by Robert's younger brother, George, the ward of Peter Freschevile who challenged the legality of Bess's marriage to Robert and refused to pay her dower.[18] As indicated in her later complaint to the Court of Chancery, early in 1545 Bess commenced proceedings for dower in the Court of Common Pleas.[19]

In mid-1546, seeking a swifter resolution, she turned to Chancery. She stated that two writs had been issued on her behalf against Freschevile but that he had deliberately prevaricated in order to 'delay and fatigue' her Common Pleas proceedings which she could no longer afford to continue. She was willing to settle the dispute for 40 marks (£26 13 s. 4d.) [20] Eventually, Bess did secure her Barley dower—paid for life—but it was never a sum on which to create a dynasty.

Quoting from Sir William Cavendish's pocketbook Arthur Collins informs us that the marriage of Sir William and Bess took place a little over six months after Edward VI's accession, at 2:00 am on 20 August 1547 at Bradgate Park, the Leicestershire home of Henry Grey, Marquis of Dorset,[21] with consummation following shortly thereafter. Grey's wife, Frances, was the daughter of Charles Brandon and his wife Mary, dowager queen of France, Henry VIII's sister. Frances was therefore the cousin of Henry VIII's daughters, Mary and Elizabeth, and his son, Edward. In 1551, following the death from sweating sickness of the two sons of his father-in-law, Grey became Duke of Suffolk.

By 1545, Henry and Frances Grey had three daughters under five. Only six months older than Prince Edward, Lady Jane Grey was born in October 1537, her parents then being just 20 and 21 years of age. The year 1540 saw the birth of Jane's sister, Katherine, and the youngest of the Grey sisters, Mary, was born in 1545. That same year Bess commenced her Barley dower proceedings.

Sir William's marriage to Bess took place at the Grey's principal county seat but little is known about this period of Bess's life. Henry and Frances and their daughters Jane and Katherine stood as godparents to one or more of Sir William and Bess's children. Henry was godfather to their sons Henry and Charles. Their first child, Frances, was christened in honour of her godmother, Frances Grey. Their first son, Henry, was almost certainly named for Henry Grey.

Sir William and Bess's second son, William, if not named after his father, may well have been named for William Parr and their third son Charles was probably named for Charles Brandon. Along with her mother, Jane Grey stood as godmother to Sir William and Bess's second daughter, Temperance, and Katherine Grey was godmother to their daughter Elizabeth.[22] Bess and Sir William's daughter, Mary, was probably named for Sir William's unmarried half-sister who lived with Sir William and Bess at Northaw and who died at Chatsworth in 1556, the same year as their daughter Mary was born.

Bess was of a similar age to Frances Grey. A portrait of 'my lady Jane' listed at Chatsworth in the 1560s is believed to have been kept by Bess on her bedside table.[23] It has been claimed Jane and Katherine Grey were bridesmaids at Sir William's marriage to Bess.[24] Bess is said to have cherished a ring given to her by Frances Grey. Although there is no definitive contemporary evidence proving Bess entered the service of the Greys at Bradgate the weight of circumstantial evidence suggests that Bess joined the Grey household in 1545 coinciding with the birth of Mary the youngest of the Grey sisters. It may have been on the advice of the Greys, or Sir William Cavendish, that Bess turned to Chancery to settle her claim for dower in the Barley estate.[25]

Henry Marmion, gent, crops up at various stages in the story of the Hardwicks. Together with John Leake, he was an executor of John Hardwick's will and remained close to the Hardwicks after John's death in 1528. John's son and heir, James, was around three years of age when his father died and thus subject to wardship. In March 1530, James's wardship was sold by the Court of Wards for £20 to a minor courtier named John Bugby. Probably with a degree of conventional exaggeration, in 1533 Bugby claimed he had been forcibly evicted from Hardwick Hall by a gang of men led by John Leake and Marmion.[26] Around 1540 Marmion appears to have masterminded an alleged attack at Chatsworth for which he, Bess's mother and others, were brought before the Derby assizes and later investigated by Star Chamber.[27]

Henry Marmion was a senior servant of the Willoughbys of Wollaton. There were long-standing connections between the Hardwicks and the Willoughbys.[28] Sir Henry Willoughby married Anne Grey, the sister of Henry Grey of Bradgate. Sir Henry and Anne had a daughter, Margaret, and two sons, Thomas, and Francis. Anne died in 1548 and following their father's death in 1549 the two boys were subject to wardship.

Francis, aged three, became the ward of his maternal uncle, Henry Grey. On Thomas's death in 1559, the Willoughby estates passed to Francis who as Sir Francis Willoughby was to become the builder of Wollaton Hall. It is very possible that Bess's long association with Sir Francis Willoughby may have begun at Bradgate. Bess was twenty-three years old when she became a widow for the first time.

The bequests made to Bess in her father's will were spent and given his own financial difficulties it is likely that Ralph Leche did not wish to incur the costs of her return to the family home. The Willoughbys were regular visitors to Bradgate. It is very possible Bess entered into service with the Greys at the intercession of Henry Marmion with Lady Willoughby, Henry Grey's sister.

William Cavendish's career as a bureaucrat began in the 1520s. Possibly on the recommendation of his elder brother George, around 1530 he entered the service of Thomas Cromwell.[29] William's entry into Cromwell's service coincided with Wolsey's fall and the beginning of his new master's meteoric rise to power during the 1530s. It was likely to Cromwell that Sir William owed his introductions to both the Greys and the Seymours. Cavendish owned a picture of 'Lord Cromwell' and among the portraits in the Long Gallery at Hardwick Hall is a rare painting of Edward Seymour. This portrait was probably among those known to have been owned by Sir William at his home at Northaw.[30]

Edward Seymour was the elder brother of Henry VIII's third wife, Jane Seymour, mother of Prince Edward. Along with Edward Seymour, Cromwell encouraged Henry VIII's courtship and marriage to Jane. Cromwell's son, Gregory, became the second husband of Queen Jane's sister, Elizabeth Seymour. It was probably as a servant of Cromwell that Cavendish came to the attention of Edward Seymour, who in 1536 appointed William to the post of auditor of the newly created Court of Augmentations. William spent much of the following three years in the Home Counties and the Midlands receiving the surrender of religious houses.[31] During this time, he must have developed a wide network of associates and contacts.

Cavendish was knighted in 1546 and sat as MP for Thirsk in the 1547 parliament. The seat was in the gift of either Cromwell's former protege Robert Holgate, archbishop of York and President of the Council of the North, or the borough's lord, Edward Stanley, 3rd Earl of Derby. Despite his later apostasy, at this time Holgate was a supporter of evangelical reform, whereas Stanley was rightly suspected of being Catholic. It may have been Edward Seymour who recommended Cavendish to Holgate.[32] Sir William was also an associate of Seymour's steward, Sir John Thynne of Longleat, at one point seeking Sir John's help to find a plasterer for Chatsworth,[33] a request Bess repeated in 1560.[34]

In 1553, Thynne became comptroller of Princess Elizabeth's household. Sir William was an associate of the Greys who, in turn, were closely allied to Seymour, to Catherine Parr's brother William, and to John Dudley. At the time of his marriage to Bess, Cavendish was renting his London house in Aldersgate from Parr.[35] Sir William's first wife, Margaret Bostock, died in 1540. Although the marriage produced two surviving daughters, Cavendish lacked a male heir. Perhaps he cast an eye over Bess at Bradgate yet it is also possible that his eye may have been steered in Bess's direction by the Greys.

Following Henry VIII's death, in January 1547, Edward Seymour used his position as the boy-king's uncle to establish himself as Lord Protector of England and Governor of the King's Person. By the end of March 1547, he had also taken for himself the title of Duke of Somerset, a title with royal connotations having been held previously by Henry VIII's Beaufort ancestors and by the late king's illegitimate son, Henry Fitz-Roy. There were particularly close connections between the Greys and the Seymours. Henry Grey and Edward Seymour had known each other from boyhood and, along with William Parr, served in Fitz-Roy's household.[36]

In February 1549, Grey and Seymour discussed a possible marriage between Lady Jane Grey, third in line to the throne, and Seymour's son Edward, Earl of Hertford.[37] Frances Grey's mother died in June 1533 and three months later her father, Charles Brandon, married his ward, the 14-year-old Katherine Willoughby, and took control of her family's extensive properties in Lincolnshire and elsewhere.[38] Katherine would later become the patron and protector of bible translator Myles Coverdale.

In the early months of 1547, Edward Seymour's younger brother, Thomas, 1st Lord Sudeley, married Henry VIII's widow, Catherine Parr. Thomas resented his elder brother's influence over their nephew, Edward VI, and envied the power that came with this influence. Although promoted to the rank of Lord High Admiral, he felt strongly that the offices of Lord Protector and Governor of the King's Person should not have been held by the same person. As the king's other uncle, he took the view that the latter position rightly belonged to him. Despite the opposition of Frances Grey and the unease of her husband, Thomas had persuaded Henry Grey to allow the ten-year-old Lady Jane Grey to join his household by promising to promote a marriage between Jane and the king.[39]

Rumours spread that Thomas intended to marry Jane but his sights were set on a greater prize. Shortly before his marriage to Catherine, Thomas offered his hand in marriage to the king's sister, Princess Elizabeth.[40] Elizabeth declined his proposal but for a while was placed in the Admiral's household. His flirting with and other improper advances towards the princess so alarmed Catherine that she had Elizabeth moved elsewhere. Following Catherine's death Thomas was suspected of seeking to renew his suit with the princess.[41]

Edward Seymour had been infuriated by his brother's marriage to Catherine and thereafter relations between the brothers deteriorated further. By early 1549, intense jealousy of his brother finally drove Thomas to seek to gain control of Edward VI. Arrested on suspicion of plotting to kidnap the king, he was found guilty of treason and executed in March 1549.[42] Things also went badly for Somerset. The Lord Protector consistently ignored William Paget's warnings that many members of the Privy Council resented his autocratic style of government.[43]

By October 1549, Seymour was under arrest and the Protectorate was at an end. Among those placed in the Tower for being 'principal instruments and counsellors… in the affairs of his (Seymour's) ill government' was Sir John Thynne.[44] Seymour's position as Lord Protector had been ratified on the final day of the 1547 parliament. Two years later Edward VI noted in his journal that by another Act of Parliament, "The Lord Protector lost, by his own agreement and submission, his protectorship, treasurership, marshalship, all his moveables and nearly £2,000 worth of land."[45]

When Mary Tudor commenced her rebellion against Queen Jane in 1553 John Dudley, Duke of Northumberland, and William Parr, Marquis of Northampton, led the party sent to Norfolk to arrest her. As it became clear that the scheme to keep Jane on the throne was doomed many, including almost every member of the Privy Council, abandoned her cause and blamed the entire affair on Dudley. Cavendish certainly had an affinity with those who sought to place Jane Grey on the throne and with the principals of the Wyatt rebellion. A portrait of Wyatt is listed in the Hardwick inventory of 1601.[46] Wyatt was yet another of Thomas Cromwell's proteges and Sir William is likely to have met him after entering Cromwell's service.

Although there is no documentary evidence to show that Sir William participated in the attempt to prevent Mary Tudor's succession or that he had any involvement in the Wyatt rebellion, his affinities, his circle, and his position as a senior official suggest that he must at least have been aware of events. Changing sides in the interest of self-preservation was a powerful motivator in an age in which a likely alternative was losing one's head on the block. William Paulet, Earl of Wiltshire, William Cecil, and Henry Grey, for example, had little hesitation switching allegiance from Somerset to Dudley,[47] and Sir John Thynne, among others, found no difficulty proclaiming Mary Tudor queen on the realisation that the Jane Grey episode was at an end.[48]

During the spring of 1551, Somerset was joined by the earls of Shrewsbury, Arundel and Derby in an alleged plot to overthrow Dudley. The main objective of the plot appears to have been the assassination of Dudley. A botched attempt on Dudley's life led to Arundel's arrest. Shrewsbury and Derby looked to distance themselves from the whole affair.[49] Somerset's role in the conspiracy led to his trial and execution, although much of the evidence against him came from yet another turncoat, his former servant and Dudley acolyte Sir Thomas Palmer who was later to confess that much of the evidence he had given against Somerset had been fabricated.

Mary Tudor's successful revolt against Queen Jane resulted in pretty much the entire Privy Council abandoning John Dudley to his fate.[50] Others, such as Sir John Thynne and Sir John Bonham, stated that the forces at their command had been raised for Mary's defence. Cavendish was to claim he had spent 1,000 marks raising men on Mary's behalf.[51] Though there is no evidence to the contrary, his Protestant leanings, close association with the Greys and members of their affinity make this seem dubious.

Sir William's career was far more likely to have prospered had Jane remained on the throne rather than—as events were to prove—with Mary as queen. Mary may have been inclined to show mercy to Jane but Henry Grey's involvement with the Wyatt Rebellion sealed his and daughter's fate. Lady Jane and Guildford Dudley were executed on 12 February 1554, and her father's head was placed on the execution block eleven days later. Wyatt's execution followed on 11 April.

However, it was neither feasible nor practical for Mary to dispose of her entire civil service in this way. It was probably Dudley who had blocked Cavendish's bid to become sheriff of Nottinghamshire and Derbyshire in November 1552, and it was possibly because he was not known to have been a close associate of Dudley that Sir William was among those who successfully sued for a general pardon and managed to survive in the aftermath of the Jane Grey affair.[52] Unlike several other senior officials,[53] he retained his office of Treasurer of the Chamber but in a diminished capacity receiving far fewer Privy Council warrants under Mary, suggesting that he was never fully trusted by the new Queen. It has been said that during his later years, Sir William spent more time on domestic matters than professional ones.[54]

In April 1557, an investigation was ordered into his accounts.[55] It was alleged that he owed the crown £5,237 5 s. He admitted the debt and at the same time asked the Privy Council to show mercy to Bess and their children.[56] In July 1556 he was at Chatsworth from where he wrote to Sir John Thynne saying he was suffering from his 'olde desease and syoknes'. He died aged 49 in October 1557, Bess praying to the Lord 'to ridd mee and his poore Children of our great Misserie'.[57] When a bill for the recovery of Sir William's debt was introduced into parliament one of the first people Bess turned to for help was her 'very good friend' Sir John Thynne.[58]

Historians have not examined sufficiently the question of how these momentous events may have influenced Sir William's decisions to marry Bess and relocate to Derbyshire. The early stirrings of the most serious rebellion of Henry VIII's reign, the 1536 Pilgrimage of Grace, began west of the Pennines in Lancashire but quickly spread into Yorkshire and Lincolnshire. In the aftermath of the rebellion, the king sought to impose his authority in the north and ordered

Charles Brandon to transfer the main centre of his operations from Suffolk to Lincolnshire. By the time of his death in 1545, Brandon had laid the foundations of a major aristocratic anti-Catholic affinity and his leadership role within it passed to his son-in-law Henry Grey the then Marquis of Dorset. Composed predominantly of supporters of evangelical reform and the Edwardian Reformation, this affinity formed a substantial bloc of powerful anti-Catholic opposition in the region.

Its members included the Greys (Leicestershire, Lincolnshire, Staffordshire), the Willoughbys (Nottinghamshire, Lincolnshire, Staffordshire, Warwickshire), William Parr, Marquis of Northampton (Lord Lieutenant of Cambridgeshire, Northamptonshire, Bedfordshire, Huntingdonshire and Norfolk) and Francis, 5th Earl of Shrewsbury (Yorkshire, Derbyshire, Nottinghamshire, Staffordshire). It was an affinity well represented among the godparents of Sir William and Bess's children. In addition to the Greys, these included numerous members of the Greys' Protestant circle. Katherine Brandon (nee Willoughby), dowager Duchess of Suffolk, and her son the young Henry, Duke of Suffolk, were two of the three godparents to Sir William's first child by Bess.

The marchioness of Northampton, the 5th Earl of Shrewsbury, the earl and countess of Warwick, the Earl of Pembroke, and the Princess Elizabeth all became godparents to one or other of Sir William and Bess's children. Doubtless political expediency and pragmatism led to Mary Tudor and Stephen Gardiner joining Henry Grey as godparents to Sir William and Bess's fifth child, Charles, born early in Mary's reign. However, this did not deter the Cavendishes from reverting to their choice of Greys and Parrs as godparents to their sixth child, Elizabeth.[59]

Beneath the greater aristocratic affinities lay local connections. Intermarriage between neighbouring gentry families had made relatives of Leakes, Hardwicks, Leches, Boswells, Chaworths, Barleys, Markhams, Foljambes and Frescheviles. Attempting to make sense of contemporary political coteries, a manuscript book of pedigrees, probably drawn up at Haddon in the 1560s, [60] links families together in genealogical groupings. One of these groups is 'linea leeke gray et frechvyle'. Bess is included on account of her descent via her mother from the Leakes of Cotham and the Greys of Sandiacre.

Other Derbyshire and Nottinghamshire families linked in this way include the Cartwrights, Watertons, Merings, Foljambes, Tempests, Barleys and Cliftons. Among the Catholic families of Derbyshire were the Babingtons of Dethick, the

FitzHerberts of Padley and the Eyres of Hassop. The Eyres supported Catholic enclaves at Hope, Dunston, Newbold and Hathersage. From the late fifteenth century much of Derbyshire no longer came under the control of any great magnate.[61] This meant that should there be any Catholic opposition to the reformation of religion during the reigns of Henry VIII and Edward VI north Derbyshire formed a potentially vulnerable area within an otherwise extensive central block of territory controlled by the Grey affinity.

A potential weak link in the affinity was the conservative Francis, 5th Earl of Shrewsbury. Although he had loyally done his part to put down the Pilgrimage of Grace, he was known to be sympathetic to Catholicism and lukewarm towards reform. The 1536 Pilgrimage of Grace had in part spread through Talbot's main Yorkshire territories and coincided with the dissolution of the lesser monasteries in Derbyshire and elsewhere. In addition to Brandon's relocation to Lincolnshire, in October 1537, none other than the Lord Privy Seal, Thomas Cromwell, now armed with the powers of his recently acquired offices of Vice Gerent Over Spirituals and Vicar General, was added to the Derbyshire commission of the peace, 'his first known commission outside lowland England'.[62] The dissolution of Derbyshire's greater monasteries followed between 1538 and 1540.

Was Sir William Cavendish's marriage to Bess in 1547 part of an attempt by Henry Grey to plant a trustworthy ally in north Derbyshire? If so, was Bess merely a pawn in the hands of the Greys? Marriage to the daughter of a long-established north-east Derbyshire gentry family, the niece of another, the widow of a third, and whose brother-in-law and stepfather's family had recently been the owners of Chatsworth, would have ensured Sir William's ready acceptance in the county following his relocation to Derbyshire. Bess's mother, Elizabeth, was the daughter of Thomas Leake of Hasland, younger brother of Sir John Leake of Sutton. Bess was the widow of Robert Barley of Barlow Lees. By the mid-1540s, her sister, Jane, had married Godfrey Boswell of Gunthwaite in south Yorkshire. Their only son Francis died childless about 1563 and their four daughters all married into other Yorkshire gentry families.

Another sister, Alice, married Francis Leche of Chatsworth who, in retaliation for his wife's infidelity, in 1547 rashly sold the estates of Chatsworth and Cromford to Thomas Agard. Like Cavendish, Agard had been in Thomas Cromwell's service and was a client of Thomas Seymour. When Leche attempted to get back the properties he had sold, the Lord High Admiral gave his support to Agard. Leche went one better and appealed directly to Somerset who ordered that Agard could not deny the Leche family's right to inherit the properties. Thomas Agard died whilst this dispute was in progress and two years later his son, Francis Agard, brought the whole business to an end by selling the two manors to Sir William Cavendish.[63]

The timing of Sir William's marriage to Bess and his relocation to Derbyshire were indeed significant. Within weeks of the collapse of Somerset's Protectorate in the autumn of 1549, Sir William purchased the manors of Chatsworth and Cromford, after which he followed 'a policy of buying lands in Derbyshire on a considerable scale'.[64] Somerset was restored to the Privy Council on 10 April 1550 but failed to learn the lessons of 1549. He looked to regain his powers but in doing so alarmed John Dudley, Earl of Warwick, and his supporters. Somerset was arrested on largely trumped-up charges, tried and found guilty.[65]

Following in the footsteps of his younger brother, he was executed in January 1552. After the end of Somerset's Protectorate, Dudley, as Duke of Northumberland, took over the reins of government together with the office of Grand Master of the King's Household, a role which incorporated the position of Lord President of the Council. Sir William Cavendish's parliamentary career ended in April 1552, with the close of the final session of the 1547 parliament, and just weeks after Somerset's execution Cavendish took the final steps in his move to Derbyshire. In June 1552, a mere six months after Somerset's death, Sir William sold Northaw and other holdings in southern England and a few in Wales to the Crown in exchange for mainly former monastic properties, including several in Derbyshire. His office still required his presence in the capital, and he was therefore obliged to retain a London residence, a house in Brentford he rented from Sir John Thynne, but he also began to hold local offices in Derbyshire.[66]

The 'planting' of Protestant families in the Midlands may have been aided by the distribution of former monastic lands. In 1546, during the minority of Henry, 2nd Earl of Rutland, the Manners family surrendered their Northumberland estates in return for the Crown writing off their debt for the purchases of the Leicestershire priories of Belvoir and Croxton.[67] In 1547, Somerset exchanged various properties with the Crown for others nearer his estates in Somerset, Dorset and Oxfordshire, building up a substantial block of territory in the west of England.[68] Such exchanges, particularly of former monastic estates, not only helped to consolidate holdings but may also have been part of a centrally driven effort to systematically redraw the political and religious map of England.

Edward VI died in July 1553, presumably in the knowledge that the terms of his 'devise for the succession'[69] would be implemented and that he would be succeeded by Jane Grey. Among many bequests, the king left £200 to Sir William.[70] Cavendish had been a good and loyal servant to both Edward and the king's uncle, the Duke of Somerset. Furthermore, he was a member of the Grey Affinity and a supporter of religious reform.[71] At the time of Edward VI's death, the establishment of Sir William Cavendish in north Derbyshire was well in hand.

Although Henry Grey had been a close friend of Somerset, he recognised that he needed to be on good terms with the Lord President. Newly elevated as Duke of Suffolk he distanced himself from the policies of the former Protector by playing a principal role in Somerset's trial and execution. Along with William Parr and William Herbert, now Earl of Pembroke, Grey became strongly associated with Dudley's government and was among the signatories of Edward VI's 'devise'. Early in 1553 Parr's wife, Elizabeth Brooke, appears to have brokered Jane Grey's marriage to Dudley's son, Guildford. In what became a triple wedding, Jane's sister Katherine married Henry Herbert, son of the Earl of Pembroke, and Guildford's sister, another Katherine, married Francis Hastings, son of the Earl of Huntingdon.[72]

Grey and Parr were the leading players in the attempt to place Jane on the throne.[73] Among those who were for Jane was Sir John St Loe.[74] He would have become Bess's father-in-law had he not died a few months before his son William married Bess in August 1559. Sir John was another member of the wider Grey affinity. The St Loes were also members of a West Country affinity which included the Seymours, Herberts, earls of Pembroke, the Courtenays, marquises of Exeter, the Bayntons and the Thynnes.

Sir John St Loe was to become a thorn in the side of the Marian regime. He had held office under Henry VIII and in 1539 became a Groom of the Privy Chamber. Like Sir Edward Baynton, Sir John was a staunch evangelical Protestant. He was appointed a commissioner for the dissolution of chantries in Somerset. At the time of the Jane Grey affair, he was ordered by the Privy Council to muster forces in support of Jane. He had joined forces with Thynne at Longleat when Sir Nicholas Poyntz arrived with the news that Mary Tudor had been proclaimed queen in London. Thynne had no other option than to proclaimed Mary queen and did so at Warminster. St Loe rode to Somerset with like intent.[75] A letter arrived in Nottinghamshire from Bradgate ordering the assembled forces at Wollaton to be stood down.[76] Sir John St Loe remained active in local government but no longer attended court during Mary's reign.

In 1556, a group of Protestant conspirators led by Sir Henry Dudley and Edward Courtney, Marquis of Exeter, sought French help to drive Queen Mary into exile in Spain and place Princess Elizabeth on the throne. Suspected of being involved in the plot, Sir John's second son, Edward, was committed to the Fleet prison. Sir John was placed under house arrest at his London home. He died in March 1559.[77]

Sir John St Loe was the father of Bess's third husband, Sir William St Loe. By 1538, William was in the service of Edward Courtenay, second cousin to Edward VI. Courtenay was yet another principal of the Wyatt rebellion for which he spent a spell in the Tower before being released in 1555 due to a lack of evidence to convict him. Knighted under Seymour in 1549, following the death of Edward VI Sir William became a member of Princess Elizabeth's household. He was involved in the Wyatt rebellion and is known to have carried at least one message from Wyatt to the princess.

Sir William was arrested, placed in the Tower and in June 1554 transferred to the Fleet prison. After paying £200 as surety for his future good conduct, like Courtenay, he was released in 1555. He was to perform an important role as Captain of the Queen's Guard at Elizabeth I's coronation and became Chief Butler of England. He sat in Elizabeth's second parliament as an MP for Derbyshire and became a JP for the county. He settled Bess's debt to the Crown, reduced to £1,000 by Queen Elizabeth. He died in December 1565. At the time of his death, his brother, Edward, was in London, the brothers being engaged in a bitter dispute over the future of their father's estates.[78]

If there was a scheme to plant Cavendish in Derbyshire, its continuing success was brought to a temporary halt by his death in 1557. Bess's third husband, Sir William St Loe, was himself part of the wider Grey affinity. Should Sir William die without issue, his heir was his brother Edward who along with their sister Elizabeth had been excluded from their father's will.[79] Sir William's first wife was Jane Baynton (c1521-1549) daughter of Sir Edward Baynton. Neighbours of the St Loes, the Thynnes and the Seymours and the Bayntons were the largest landowners in the area and supporters of evangelical reform. Sir Edward became vice-chamberlain to Anne Boleyn and Catherine Howard. He was also a close ally of Hugh Latimer.[80] Both Sir Edward and Sir John St Loe were among the guests at the christening of Edward VI.[81]

Sir William's marriage to Jane took place no later than 1538. Jane died in 1549. It is unclear whether the marriage produced offspring. There is no entry for the St Loe family in the 1565 Herald's visitation of Wiltshire. However, the Baynton entry states Jane had two daughters and implies that these were Sir William's daughters. The 1623 Wiltshire visitation record does include an entry for the St Loes which states clearly that when Sir William died in 1565, he died without issue.[82] Having conceived eight times during her ten years of marriage to Cavendish, Bess had amply demonstrated her fecundity. Perhaps St Loe hoped Bess would provide him with an heir. But, if he needed an heir, why would he have waited a decade before his second marriage?

Edward St Loe appears to have been sufficiently alarmed at the prospect of his brother's marriage to Bess producing an heir that he allegedly turned to desperate measures to prevent it. In addition to claims of the use of sorcery, in a letter to Bess dated June 1560, the brothers' stepmother, Margaret St Loe, claimed that she had been informed by an anonymous lady that shortly after St Loe's marriage Edward had attempted to poison both Bess and his brother. The accusation of attempted murder was investigated but presumably due to a lack of evidence, substance or both, Edward was never convicted of the offence. St Loe's marriage to Bess proved childless.

It has been claimed that Edward's alleged attempt to commit double murder so embittered Sir William that, despite Bess's reluctance, in his will, Sir William left all his lands, possessions and wealth, to her. He was free to do so because the lands had not been settled after his father's death.[83] By cutting out Edward and their sister Elizabeth from his will, Sir William was merely reaffirming the provisions of their father's will.[84]

Twice widowed, with six children to bring up and a huge debt hanging over her head, Bess might not have been considered the most attractive prospect for a bride. On the other hand, William St Loe must have been an attractive prospect as a husband. In order to explain why he married Bess, various authors have argued that like Cavendish before him, St Loe simply loved her, a conclusion based mainly on the expressions of love and affection he used in the small number of his letters that survive.[85] However, caution must be exercised when interpreting such expressions as being matters of fact rather than of convention.[86] The St Loes were well known to Sir William Cavendish and Bess through his associations with Edward Seymour, the Greys, the Parrs, the Thynnes and others both inside and outside court circles.

Sir William's marriage to Margaret Bostock (d.1540) had produced two surviving daughters. Catherine and Anne. Catherine married Thomas Brooke, son of Lord Cobham, whose sister, Elizabeth, was William Parr's second wife. Anne married Henry Baynton, brother of Sir William St Loe's first wife, Jane Baynton.[87] William Cavendish was therefore related by marriage to the St Loes sometime before his marriage to Bess which indicates that William St Loe and Bess must have known each other long before they married in 1559. Bess maintained her links with the Bayntons: another Anne Baynton was a beneficiary of Bess's will.

Bess faced a desperate situation at the time of her marriage to St Loe. Possibly encouraged by Sir John Thynne, Sir William's marriage to Bess may have been little more than an act of kindness by one old friend to another. St Loe and Bess spent relatively little time together during their six-year marriage. Sir William's position at court necessitated his presence in London whereas Bess spent much of their marriage at Chatsworth. However, St Loe's marriage to Bess helped to re-establish the Grey affinity's presence in Derbyshire.

The wedding of Lady Katherine Grey to Somerset's son, Edward, Earl of Hertford, in December 1560 took place during the period of the St Loe marriage and reflected the continuing concerns of the Grey affinity, now headed by George Talbot, 6th Earl of Shrewsbury. No one could predict how long Elizabeth might reign. Should she die without issue Katherine was a potential successor. Elizabeth's near death from smallpox on 15 October 1562,[88] was a sharp reminder, if one was needed, that the threat of a Catholic succession had not entirely evaporated with Queen Mary's death.

This concern may also have been a factor in Bess's fourth marriage to George Talbot, whose family was closely aligned with the Greys, Willoughbys, Parrs, Herberts and other leading members of the affinity. Talbot's father, Francis, 5th Earl of Shrewsbury, was among the signatories of Edward VI's 'devise'[89] but was not closely allied to Northumberland. In 1562, the 6th earl's eldest son, Francis, Lord Talbot, married Anne, daughter of William Herbert, 1st Earl of Pembroke, and Anne Parr, sister of Catherine Parr. Within months of Bess becoming widowed for the third time court gossip buzzed with rumours of potential suitors, Sir John Thynne, Lord Darcy and Sir Henry Cobham, being the main contenders,[90] but within a few months of the death of his first wife, Gertrude Manners, George Talbot, 6th Earl of Shrewsbury, married Bess.

Unlike Cavendish and St Loe, there can be no suggestion of the earl needing a male heir as he already had his 'heir and spare' in Francis, Lord Talbot, and Gilbert Talbot. He was vastly wealthier than Bess. Adding her wealth to his own cannot have been the sole motive for their marriage. He may have wanted to prevent anyone else from having any influence in the region. The earl would have had control of Bess's Cavendish and St Loe estates during their marriage, but Bess held only a life interest in the Cavendish lands, which had been settled mainly on Henry Cavendish in 1557, and her St Loe estates passed to Charles Cavendish.

As with the St Loe's marriage, Talbot's marriage to Bess made perfect sense in that it served to maintain the political and religious status quo in north-east Derbyshire that had been established in 1547 by the Greys via Sir William Cavendish's marriage to Bess. Mary, Queen of Scots, was not placed in the custody of George Talbot in 1569 solely because he was a person of great wealth, nor just because Mary would be held at properties far distant from court, but also because by that time Talbot had become the leading member of a significant Protestant affinity, the origins of which lay in the extension of royal authority following the Pilgrimage of Grace and on which Elizabeth and her government believed they could depend.

E. W. Ives dedicated his biography of Lady Jane Grey to his students and 'many friends who have grappled with the reign of Edward VI'. Finding one's way through the maze of high politics during the mid-sixteenth century remains challenging. Following the failure to place Jane on the throne, many of the leaders of the attempt, such as Henry Grey, escaped with their lives, at least for the time being. Shamelessly yet pragmatically, former allies left John Dudley[91] to his fate on Tower Hill where he was beheaded in August 1553. Early in Elizabeth's reign an anonymous account characterised Somerset as the 'good duke' and Northumberland as his evil counterpart.[92]

Dudley became a scapegoat and dead men cannot defend themselves. Inevitably, much that could have been used to convict others disappeared at the time, shortly afterwards or in the years that followed. Sir William Cavendish had witnessed first-hand the fall of powerful men such as Wolsey, Cromwell, and Somerset. Men like Cavendish, operating a tier or so below the principal members of the aristocratic affinities they served, were clever, astute, careful, and cautious. They understood the danger that letters and papers might pose in any given circumstance, and they were adept at covering their tracks.

Thus far, it has proved impossible to discover documentary evidence of any involvement many such men may have had in events such as the attempt to prevent Mary Tudor's accession and her marriage to Philip of Spain. We should not be surprised by this paucity of evidence and accept that much must be inferred. Conclusions reached in these circumstances are necessarily speculative yet remain worthy of consideration.

Placing Sir William Cavendish's marriage to Bess against the backdrop of the religious, political, and economic upheavals of the mid-sixteenth century allows us to take account of previously unconsidered factors which not only help to explain the marriage itself but also Sir William's subsequent decision to relocate to Derbyshire. His move to Derbyshire was driven by religious and geo-political factors. It is an explanation in which Bess cannot be seen as a force for unbridled dynastic ambition but as a pawn in the hands of powerful aristocratic affinities.

References and Notes

[1] *The Works of Horatio Walpole, Earl of Orford* (London, 1798), IV, 206. My thanks are extended to Peter Foden, my friend and former colleague, Lesley A. Bilby and to Philip Riden, for helpful comments and proof-reading skills.

[2] Sir William Dugdale, *Baronage of England* (London, 1675-6), 420.

[3] E. Lodge, *Illustrations of British History* (London, 1838), I, p. xxviii.

[4] T. Kilburn, 'The wardship and marriage of Robert Barley, first husband of Bess of Hardwick', *Derbyshire Archaeological Journal*, 134 (2014), 197-203.

[5] P. Riden, 'Sir William Cavendish: Tudor civil servant and founder of a dynasty', *Derbyshire Archaeological Journal*, 129 (2009), 248.

[6] Ibid, 224.

[7] A. Collins, *Historical Collections of the Noble Families of Cavendishe, Holles, Vere, Harley, and Ogle* (London, 1752), 22.

[8] Ibid, 10; Riden, 'Cavendish', 224.

[9] D. MacCulloch, *Thomas Cromwell: A Life* (London: Allen Lane, 2018), 549.

[10] The National Archives (TNA) STAC 3/1/49.

[11] Riden, 'Cavendish', 245.

[12] A.C. Jones, 'Commotion Time: The English risings of 1549' (Unpublished PhD thesis, University of Warwick, 2003), 33-4, 40 n. 22.

[13] Riden, 'Cavendish', 247.

[14] J. Loach and R. Tittler (eds), *Problems in Focus: The Mid-Tudor Polity, c.1540-1560* (London: MacMillan, 1980) provides a useful introduction.

[15] M. Scard, Edward Seymour, *Lord Protector: Tudor King in all but name* (Stroud: History Press, 2016), 161, 266 n. 30.

[16] Loach and Tittler (eds), Mid-Tudor Polity, 34-5; S. Alford, *The Watchers: A Secret History of the Reign of Elizabeth* I (London, Penguin Books, 2013), see, for example, 149, 183.

[17] C. Skidmore, *Edward VI: the lost king of England* (London: Weidenfeld & Nicolson, 2007), 183; J.E. Neale, *Queen Elizabeth I* (London, 1979), 378; Folger, Cavendish-Talbot MSS, X.d.428 (34).

[18] Kilburn, 'Wardship', 195.

[19] Ibid, 201, n. 17; TNA, C 1/1101/17.

[20] Kilburn, ibid, 198-9.

[21] Collins, *Historical Collections*, 11, 19.

[22] Ibid, 19-20.

[23] D. Ashead and D.A.H.B. Taylor (eds), *Hardwick Hall: a great old castle of romance* (New Haven and London: Yale University Press, 2016), 73, citing Devonshire MSS, H/143/6; Durant, 52.

[24] R. Davey. In *The Sisters of Lady Jane Grey and Their Wicked Grandfather* published in 1912, Richard Davey states the Grey sisters were bridesmaids at Sir William's marriage to Bess, However, he fails to give any reference to the source of this information.
V. Wilson, *Queen Elizabeth's Maids of Honour* (London: Bodley Head, 1922), 27.

[25] D.N. Durant, *Bess of Hardwick: Portrait of an Elizabethan Dynast* (London: Weidenfield & Nicholson, 1979), 12. There is no evidence to support Dugdale's claim that Bess entered the service of the Zouches of Codnor. There is strong circumstantial evidence that she was probably in service to the Greys; P. Riden, 'The Hardwicks of Hardwick Hall in the fifteenth and sixteenth centuries', *Derbyshire Archaeological Journal*, 130 (2010), 152. Interestingly, in the sixteenth century, a marriage ceremony usually took place at the bride's home. In the case of the marriage of Sir William Cavendish and Bess, this would appear to have been Bradgate.

[26] Riden, 'Hardwicks', 157

[27] TNA, STAC 2/17/53.

[28] Riden, 'Hardwicks' 147; E.W Ives, *Lady Jane Grey: a Tudor Mystery* (Oxford: Wiley-Blackwell, 2011), 36. Even allowing for the importance of extended family relationships in the sixteenth century the suggestion that Bess's link to the Greys came about via her association with the Marmions and the Willoughbys is, in my view, much more plausible than the notion that it was due to Bess's distant relationship to the Greys of Sandiacre.

[29] Riden, 'Cavendish', 239; Bath Mss, Thynne Mss. 2, ff. 250-253v.; *History of Parliament. Commons 1509-58*, Sir William Cavendish.

[30] G. White, "that whycheysnedefoulle and nesesary": the nature and purpose of the original furnishing and decoration of Hardwick Hall' (Unpublished PhD thesis, University of Warwick, 2005), 293, 468.

[31] Riden, 'Cavendish', 239-40.

[32] *History of Parliament. Commons 1509-58*, Sir William Cavendish.

[33] Durant, *Bess of Hardwick: portrait of an Elizabethan dynast*, 26-7.

[34] Ibid, 47.

[35] Ibid, 16.

[36] Scard, Seymour, 17.

[37] Ives, Jane Grey, 43-5.

[38] S. Gunn, *Charles Brandon: Henry VIII's closest friend* (Stroud: Amberley, 2015), 157.

[39] Ives, *Jane Grey*, 184.

[40] Scard, *Seymour*, 119-20.

[41] Neale, *Elizabeth I*, ch. 2; Scard, *Seymour*, 120-5; J. Loach, *Edward VI* (New Haven and London: Yale University Press, 1999), 56-7.

[42] Neale, Elizabeth 1, 29-33.

[43] D.E. Hoak, *The King's Council in the Reign of Edward VI* (Cambridge: Cambridge University Press, 1976), 96-7; Scard, *Seymour*, 74, 154; S.R. *Gammon, Statesman and Schemer: William First Lord Paget, Tudor Minister* (Newton Abbot: David & Charles, 1973), 152.

[44] *History of Parliament. Commons 1558-1603*, John Thynne.

[45] Beer. B.L, 'Edward, duke of Somerset [known as Protector Somerset] (c.1500-1552)', *Oxford Dictionary of National Biography*, https://doi.org/10.1093/ref:odnb/25159; J. North (ed), *England's Boy King: the diary of Edward VI, 1547-1553* (Welwyn Garden City: Ravenhall Books, 2005), 40; Scard, *Seymour*, 124.

[46] L. Boynton, *The Hardwick Hall Inventories of 1601* (London: Furniture History Society, 1971), 29.

[47] Scard, *Seymour*, 230; Loach, *Edward VI*, 93; Skidmore, *Edward VI, 207-9*.

[48] *History of Parliament. Commons* 1558-1603, Sir John St Loe.

[49] Skidmore, *Edward VI*, 191-2; Gammon, *Statesman and Schemer'* 178-9; Scard, *Seymour*, 225.

[50] J.G. Nichols (ed.), The Chronicle of Queen Jane and Queen Mary (Camden Society, Old Series 48, 1850), 7, 10.

[51] Riden, 'Cavendish', 247; Durant, 26; Ives, Jane Grey, 220.

[52] *History of Parliament. Commons 1509-58*, Sir William Cavendish.

[53] D. Loades, *Mary Tudor* (Oxford: Blackwell, 1989), 190.

[54] *History of Parliament. Commons 1509-58*, Sir William Cavendish.

[55] TNA, E 101/424/10, *History of Parliament. Commons 1509-58*, Sir William Cavendish.

[56] Riden, 'Cavendish', 247-8.

[57] Collins, *Historical Collections*, 20.

[58] Ibid, 12.

[59] Ibid, 19-20; Durant, *Bess of Hardwick*, 20-7. If William was not named after his father a likely candidate for this honour is William Parr whose wife, Elizabeth Brooke, stood as one of William's godmothers and was godmother to Sir William and Bess's daughter Elizabeth.

[60] I am indebted to Peter Foden for advising me that in a box labelled 'pedigrees' in the Belvoir Castle Muniments, there is a book of manuscript pedigrees of c.1565. The unknown genealogist was trying to explain contemporary allegiances. Among the pedigrees is one titled 'Leeke Grey and Frechvyle'.

[61] See generally, S. M. Wright, *The Derbyshire Gentry in the Fifteenth Century* (Derbyshire Record Society, 1983).

[62] MacCulloch, *Cromwell*, 272-5, 435.

[63] Durant, *Bess*, 18-19.

[64] Ibid, 23; Riden, 'Cavendish', 245-7.

[65] Gammon, *'Statesman and Schemer'*, 179-80.

[66] Riden, 'Cavendish', 247.

[67] I am grateful to Peter Foden for this information.

[68] Scard, Seymour, 82-3.

[69] Nichols, Chronicle, 89-91; J. G. Nichols (ed.), *Literary Remains of King Edward the Sixth* (Roxburghe Club, 1857), 571-3.

[70] Riden, 'Cavendish', 247.

[71] White, "that whycheysnedefoulle and nesesary", Appendix One, 1540s Inventory of Northaw, 324, among Sir William's possessions were at that time a mixture of items belonging to the catholic faith and evangelical reform including a vernacular bible, probably Coverdale's 1539 Great Bible.

[72] Ives, *Jane Grey*, 185.

[73] Loades, *Mary Tudor,* 179.

[74] *History of Parliament. Commons 1558-1603*, Sir John St Loe; Sir William St Loe; P. Riden, 'Bess of Hardwick and the St Loe Inheritance' in P. Riden and D. G. Edwards (eds), Essays in Derbyshire History Presented to Gladwyn Turbutt, *Derbyshire Record Society*, 30, 2006, 80-106.

[75] *History of Parliament. Commons 1558-1603*, Sir John St Loe, 330.

[76] W.H. Stevenson, *Report on the Manuscripts of Lord Middleton*, HMSO, 1911, 415.

[77] *History of Parliament. Commons 1558-1603*, Sir John St Loe, 260.

[78] Riden, 'St Loe inheritance', 100-102.

[79] Ibid, 95.

[80] MacCulloch, *Cromwell*, 167.

[81] https://www.british-history.ac.uk/letters-papers- hen8/vol 12/no2/320.

[82] G.W. Marshall (ed.), *The Visitation of Wiltshire*, 1623 (London: Bell, 1882), 8, 44, 37, 54; Lodge, *Illustrations*, I, p. xxviii, stated that Sir William St Loe had 'daughters by a former wife' but does not say how many daughters; Riden, 'St Loe inheritance', 98, n 7. The Baynton pedigree in the 1565 *Wiltshire Visitation*, W. Harvey (ed), 1897, 4, states that Jane Baynton had two daughters by Sir William St Loe. However, the 1623 describes Sir William as *ob. s.p.* (*obit sine prole*), that is 'died without issue' and furthermore no children are mentioned in Sir William's will. Jane died in 1549 and there is no mention of daughters other than that in the 1565 visitation. There was a ten-year gap between Jane's death and St Loe's marriage to Bess and one of seventeen years between Jane's death and the 1565 visitation was undertaken in the same year as William St Loe's death It is possible that if there had been two daughters, they may have died young. On the

other hand, Lodge and others may have confused Sir William St Loe with Sir William Cavendish who had four daughters by his first wife, Margaret Bostock, who died in 1540 possibly during childbirth. Only two of these daughters, Catherine, b.1535, and Anne, b.1540, survived into adulthood. The other two, Mary and Margaret, did not. Alternatively, it was common practice for a spouse to refer to children from a previous marriage as being their own children. St Loe referred to Bess's children as his children. At the time of his death two of Bess's daughters by Cavendish, Mary and Elizbeth, were yet to marry and it is possible that these were the two daughters that earlier authors were referring to when stating that St Loe had two daughters. The contradiction between the Baynton entry in the 1565 visitation and the St Loe entry in that of 1623 remains unresolved.

[83] TNA, PROB 11/48/200; TNA, C 3/170/13(2); Durant, Bess, 39.

[84] Riden, 'St Loe inheritance', 93; TNA, PROB 11/42B/241.

[85] See, for example, Durant, *Bess of Hardwick: Portrait of an Elizabethan Dynast,* 35.

[86] For a discussion of 'courtly love' see E. W. Ives, *Anne Boleyn* (Oxford: Blackwell, 1986), 77-110.

[87] Collins, Historical Collections, 18-19.

[88] J. Hurstfield, *Elizabeth I and the Unity of England* (Harmondsworth: Penguin, 1971), 44-55; Neale, 123.

[89] Nichols, Literary Remains, 573 and n. 42.

[90] Durant, Bess, 53.

[91] Nichols, The Chronicle of Queen Jane and Queen Mary, 7, 10.

[92] A.J.A. Malkiewicz, 'An eye-witness's account of the coup d'etat of October 1549', *English Historical Review*, 70 (1955), 600-9; C.L. Kingsford (ed), 'Two London chronicles from the collections of John Stowe', *Camden Miscellany,* 4 (Camden Society, 3rd ser, 18, 1910), 17-43; A.F, Pollard. *England Under Protector Somerset* (London: Kegan Paul, 1900); W.K, *Jordan, Edward VI: the young king* (London: Allen and Unwin,1968). B.L. Beer, *The Political Career of John Dudley, Earl of Warwick and Duke of Northumberland* (Kent State University Press, 1973) and 'Northumberland: the myth of the wicked duke and the historical John Dudley', *Albion*, 11 (1979), 1¬14; D.E. Hoak, 'Rehabilitating the duke of Northumberland: politics and political control, 1549-1553', in Loach and Tittler (eds), *Mid-Tudor Polity*, 29-51; M.L. Bush, *The Government Policy of Protector Somerset* (London: Edward Arnold, 1975), 160-161.

4. Three into Two Won't Go: Marriage and Hardwick's 'Eglantine Table'

© National Trust Images, John Hammond

In 1601, Elizabeth, Dowager Countess of Shrewsbury, had inventories drawn up of the contents of her properties including the 'old' and 'new' halls at Hardwick. 'Bess of Hardwick', as the Countess is better known to history, was by that date in her eighties and preparing to make her will.[1] There is no specific reference to an 'Eglantine Table' in the 1601 inventories but in the High Great Chamber of the new hall the inventory clerk did list 'a long table of white wood' and this is assumed to be the table now known as the 'Eglantine Table'.[2]

The 'Eglantine Table', which dates from around 1568, is still to be found in the High Great Chamber of Derbyshire's Hardwick Hall. It is often asserted that it was commissioned by Bess to commemorate three marriages: that of Bess to George Talbot, Earl of Shrewsbury, and two others involving four of their children.[3] The precise date and place of Bess's marriage to Talbot is not known.[4] All Bess's children had been fathered by her second husband, Sir William Cavendish, and the earl's six children were the issue of his first marriage to Gertrude, Lady Manners. On 9 February 1568, the earl's youngest daughter, 8-year-old Grace Talbot, was married to Bess's eldest son, Henry Cavendish, the 17-year-old heir of Sir William.

At the same time, the earl's 15-year-old second son, Gilbert, married Bess's youngest daughter, Mary Cavendish, who was 12. It has been suggested that the marriages of the children came about at Bess's instigation, but such a strategy of multiple marriages was commonplace among the Elizabethan aristocracy and had, for example, been pursued by Talbot himself in 1562 on the occasion of the marriage of his eldest son Francis which brought together the Talbot family and that of the Herberts, earls of Pembroke. Francis married Anne Herbert, eldest daughter of William Herbert, Earl of Pembroke, and Anne Parr, younger sister of Catherine Parr. At the same time, Pembroke's son and heir, Henry Herbert, married George Talbot's eldest daughter, Catherine Talbot. Gilbert and Mary's daughter, the diminutive Mary Talbot, married William Herbert, 3rd Earl of Pembroke, and became Countess of Pembroke.

The most important piece of evidence we have regarding the 'Eglantine Table' and its relationship to these marriages is the table itself. Inlaid into the top of the table are images of items such as playing cards, musical instruments, and various other pleasures and pastimes popular during the Elizabethan age. Also inlaid into the top of the table are two heraldic marriage impalements. As viewed, such impalements depict the arms of the male to the left and the female to the right. The first of the impalements depicts the arms of Talbot impaling those of Hardwick, obviously intended to represent the marriage of the earl to Bess. The second depicts the arms of Cavendish impaling those of Talbot, an unequivocal reference to the marriage of Henry Cavendish to Grace Talbot. Completely absent from the 'Eglantine Table' is any reference whatsoever to the marriage of Gilbert Talbot and Mary Cavendish.

If, as is often claimed, Hardwick's 'Eglantine Table' was indeed commissioned to commemorate 'three' marriages, why is there no heraldic marriage impalement to represent a third marriage, that of Gilbert Talbot and Mary Cavendish? Is this merely an error, an oversight, or did the very highly skilled men who crafted the table simply have a lapse of memory or was it omitted because there was insufficient space for its inclusion? There can be only one logical explanation for the omission: the 'Eglantine Table' was never intended to commemorate a third marriage. As evidenced by the two marriage impalements inlaid into the table itself, the 'Eglantine Table' was commissioned to commemorate 'two' marriages, not three. A recent suggestion that an impalement of Gilbert's marriage to Mary would duplicate one of the two existing impalements is incorrect as neither of these impalements portray Talbot impaling Cavendish.[5]

Rank and position mattered to the Elizabethans and Bess was certainly status-conscious. Among the more obvious examples of this are the huge 'ES' monograms that top Hardwick's lofty towers. Bess also chose to frame the non-aristocratic Hardwick coat of arms with heraldic supporters and to display monograms and the Hardwick arms beneath the coronet of a countess. Like the Eglantine Table, the Artemesia panel, one of which was once a set of five wall-hangings made at Chatsworth c.1573, displays impalements depicting Bess's marriage to George Talbot and Henry Cavendish's marriage to Grace Talbot.[6]

The over-mantle in the Cut Velvet Room provides a further example in its depictions of the marriage impalements of all six of Bess's surviving children, three to the left and three to the right. These are not placed in any chronological order beyond that of rank with each side being headed by one of Bess's two daughters who became countesses: Mary, Countess of Shrewsbury, and Elizabeth, Countess of Lennox. Bess continued to style herself 'Countess of Shrewsbury' until her own death on the 13th of February 1608, a confusing situation which led to both Bess and her daughter, Mary, being addressed as 'Countess of Shrewsbury' simultaneously.

We may wonder why Bess chose not to include the marriage of Gilbert Talbot and Mary Cavendish when she commissioned the table. When the three marriages took place, Gilbert's elder brother, Francis, Lord Talbot, was still alive. Married to the daughter of the Earl of Pembroke in 1562, Francis did not die until 1582. Gilbert was the 'spare' and not the 'heir'. In an Elizabethan aristocratic household, the first-born male was considered the most important followed by daughters who on marriage could be expected to attract substantial dowries.

As a 15-year-old second son, Gilbert's marriage to Mary was advantageous to both his father and Bess. It strengthened further the ties between the Talbot and Cavendish families, and it has been argued marriage to Gilbert conveniently relieved Bess of the necessity of providing Mary with a dowry. In terms of status, however, Gilbert and Mary's marriage was simply not in the same league as the marriages of Bess and her eldest son. Bess seems to have taken little interest in Gilbert until after 1582 when he became the 'heir' and not the 'spare'.

Once embedded into a narrative, it becomes notoriously difficult to dislodge historical myths. Does Hardwick's 'Eglantine Table' commemorate three marriages? Put simply, three into two won't go!

References and Notes

[1] The building of Hardwick New Hall commenced within weeks of the death of George Talbot who died on 18 November 1590. Modern biographers have taken to giving Bess's year of birth as 1527 but contemporary evidence suggests that a date of 1521/2 is more likely. For a discussion of Bess's year of birth see Philip Riden's 'The Hardwicks of Hardwick Hall in the Fifteenth and Sixteenth Centuries', *Derbyshire Archaeological Journal*, 130 (2010) 150-151.

[2] Boynton. L. (Ed), *The Hardwick Hall Inventories of 1601* (1971), 27. The inventory also refers to a long, carved and inlaid, table in the Low Great Chamber. At Hardwick Hall is an Elizabethan inlaid table the central feature of which is interestingly a single heraldic marriage impalement, that of Talbot impaling Hardwick. Though obviously representing the marriage of Bess to George Talbot, it is not known who commissioned this table.

[3] Goldring. E., 'Talbot, Elizabeth [Bess of Hardwick], Countess of Shrewsbury (1527?-1608)' *Oxford Dictionary of National Biography*, Oxford University Press, 2004 [http: //www.oxforddnb. com/view/ article/26925]: Goldring. E., 'Talbot, George, sixth earl of Shrewsbury (c. 1522-1590)', *Oxford Dictionary of National Biography*, Oxford University Press, 2004, online edn, May 20, [http://www.oxforddnb.com/view/article/26928]. Goldring states that the marriage of Bess and George Talbot took place in London on the 1st of November 1567, over three months before the marriage of the children. David Durant concludes his discussion of potential dates by stating "It is certainly safe to say that Bess and the Earl were married in the autumn of 1567…" Durant. D.N., *Bess of Hardwick: Portrait of an Elizabethan Dynast* (1977), 55-56. Mary Lovell argues that the marriage of Bess and Talbot took place after the marriages of the children sometime between the 9th of February and the 23rd of March 1568, at a place unknown. Lovell. M.S., *Bess of Hardwick, First Lady of Chatsworth* (2006) 200.

[4] In strict heraldic terms, as shields would be held on the arm and, thus, viewed by the holder from behind, the male's arms are said to be on the dexter side [right] and the female to the sinister side, [left]. When seen by the observer the male's arms would be

on the left and the female's to the right. It has recently been suggested probably by someone well-meaning that the reason there is no heraldic impalement for Gilbert Talbot's marriage to Mary Cavendish is because there would then have been two identical impalements. The table has one heraldic impalement showing, as observed, Talbot to the left impaling Hardwick to the right (i.e., George Talbot's marriage to Bess of Hardwick) and a second showing, as observed, Cavendish to the left impaling Talbot to the right (i.e., representing Henry Cavendish's marriage to Grace Talbot.) A heraldic impalement representing Gilbert's marriage to Mary would depict, as observed, Talbot to the left impaling Cavendish to the right. Thus, a heraldic impalement representing the marriage of Gilbert and Mary would not have clashed with either of the two impalements depicted on the table.

[5] Only one of the surviving four panels is dated.

[6] There is no actual evidence that Bess commissioned the table but the inclusion of the Hardwick and Cavendish arms to depict the marriage of Bess and that of her eldest son, together with the words "we stags exult to the divine" would suggest that it was probably commissioned by Bess to celebrate the success of the Cavendish family whose coat of arms includes three stags, therefore, making it perhaps less likely that the table was commissioned by Talbot.

5. Matters of Birth and Death
Bess's Tomb, Derby Cathedral

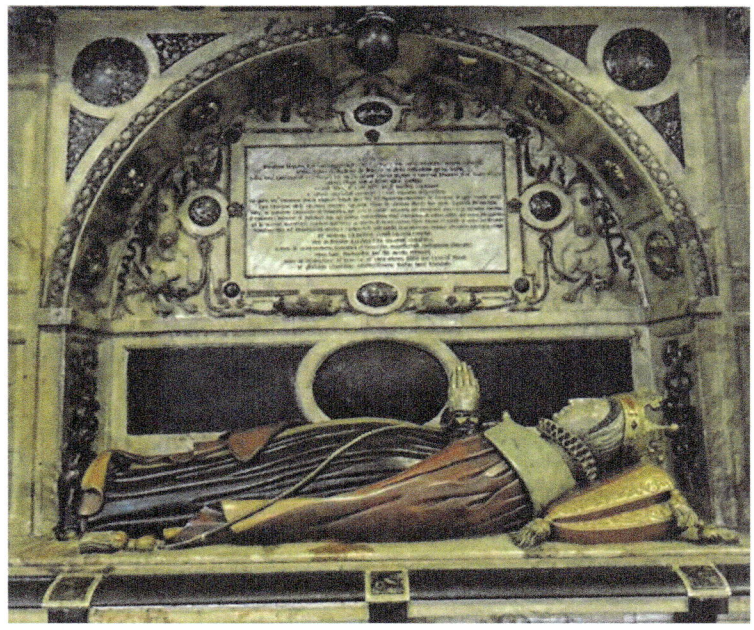

Bess's tomb, Derby Cathedral

Matters of Birth

Recent biographers have begun to argue that Bess's year of birth was 1527. This would seem to have more to do with a desire to have her move into Hardwick New Hall on her alleged seventieth birthday than it has to do with any credible historical evidence. Although an entry in the Hardwick household accounts for the 4th of October 1597 records a payment of 20s. to three of Bess's servants who played music when she moved into the new hall, there is no mention of the occasion having been her birthday, seventieth or otherwise.[1]

In his *Barlow Family Records*, Sir Montague Barlow claimed that Bess was 25 when she married Robert Barley, he does not provide any evidence to support his assertion.[2] If Bess had been 25 in 1543 then she would have to have been born in 1518. Robert Barley's date of birth is given as 10 December 1529 which generally agrees with other evidence of his birth. Arthur Collins stated that Bess was 14 in 1543 when she married Robert Barley but for that to be so she would have to have been born in 1529, which is at least a year after her father's death.[3] Collins may have confused marriage with espousal. Had Bess been 14 when she was espoused to Robert Barley in the mid-1530s then her birth year would have been 1521/22. From the late nineteenth century until recently, it was generally accepted that Bess was born in 1520.

The assertion that Bess was born in 1527 is predicated on the erroneous notion that for girls the age of 16 was the legal age of majority or coming of age. In fact, in the sixteenth century, 16 was not an age of rite of passage in either Common or Canon Law.[4] Bess's brother James was born in 1525 and entered into his inheritance when he came 'of age' in 1546, i.e. when he reached the age of 21. In their wills, testators often bequeathed legacies and provisions to daughters until they reached a given age and similar arrangements appear in marriage contracts.

However, it is important to recognise that this age could vary depending on local tradition. For example, when Gabriel Marmion agreed to marry Anne Cooper, he bound himself to pay certain sums of money to her daughters when they attained the age of 19 (see Chapter 6). However, for common law purposes in the sixteenth century the legal age of majority, the age at which men and women came of age, was 21.

In matters of litigation, a woman could not be a sole plaintiff at common law unless she was a spinster or widow and had reached the age of 21. An unmarried woman or widow, a *femme sole*, would be represented by her legal guardian until she reached the age of 21. If she did not have a guardian, the courts were empowered to nominate one to act on her behalf. John Hardwick's 1528 will named Henry Marmion and John Leake as guardians for his children. If Bess had been under 21 in 1545 she would have been represented by one of her guardians.

A married woman, or *femme covert*, would be represented by her husband. It was possible for a married woman over the age of 21 to be a sole plaintiff in a Chancery legal case. Bess's mother was the sole plaintiff in her desertion proceedings against Ralph Leche. However, by and large, the equity courts tended to follow the same procedures as the common law courts but offered swifter and cheaper judgements based on common sense rather than legal precedence.

Robert Barley died in December 1544 and the following year Bess commenced proceedings for dower in the Court of Common Pleas against Peter Freschevile and his ward, Robert's younger brother and heir George Barley. As sole plaintiff in these proceedings, she must have been at least 21 in 1545. Therefore, Bess cannot have been born any later than 1524 and this, of course, assumes she was not already over the age of 21 when she began her Common Pleas proceedings. In 1546, as sole plaintiff, Bess switched her claim for dower to the equity court of Chancery. In her initial complaint to that court, she referred to George Barley as 'being within the age of 21'[5] demonstrating once again that 21 was the age of maturity.

After Bess's marriage to Sir William Cavendish, she would have become a *femme covert* and the standard legal practice of husbands being named as plaintiffs in their wife's legal proceedings would have been employed. For example, in defending George Barley's complaint that the Barley inheritance had been subject to spoiling during his minority answer came from Sir William Cavendish and his wife Dame Elizabeth.[6]

The gentry families of north-east Derbyshire formed a distinct interconnected, interrelated and self-conscious social group. There were long-established connections and relationships between families such as the Frescheviles, Foljambes, Chaworths, Leakes, Boswells, Barleys, Columbells and Hardwicks. Bess's great, great-grandfather Roger Hardwick married Nichola Barley c1450. Robert Barley's great-grandfather was married to Eleanor Freschevile and Robert's mother was Elizabeth, daughter of James Chaworth. Robert's sister, Dorothy, married George Foljambe. In 1507, a young John Hardwick, later to become Bess's father, was conveyed property in Heath and six messuages at Hardwick by Sir Henry Willoughby of Wollaton, Ralph Greenhalgh and John Freschevile, which they had held as feoffees of Roger Hardwick.

The Hardwicks and the Frescheviles were not only close neighbours they were also close relatives. The Frescheviles would have been aware of the year of Bess's birth. Within a complex web of relationships Peter Freschevile, who claimed guardianship over Robert Barley, and Bess were second cousins. Freschevile's mother was the daughter of John Leake and Elizabeth Savage.

Bess's mother was the daughter of Thomas Leake and Margaret Fox. John and Thomas were the sons of William Leake of Sutton and Katherine Chaworth.[7]

Had Bess been under the age of 21 when she commenced legal proceedings for dower Freschevile could be expected to have lodged an objection to those proceedings on the grounds that she was within age (i.e. under 21) but no such objection appears to have been made. The record of Bess's proceedings for dower in the Court of Common Pleas is not extant. However, in her 1546 complaint to Chancery Bess informed the court that in order to obtain her dower she had been compelled to sue Freschevile in the Court of Common Pleas, proceedings she is known to have begun in that court on the 28 March 1545.[8] If Bess was the sole plaintiff in her proceedings in Common Pleas, as her initial complaint to Chancery indicates that she was, she must have already reached the age of majority by 1545 and therefore could not have been born any later than 1523/4.

In his will dated January 1528, Bess's father John Hardwick placed his children in the custody of their mother.[9] She was to receive 26s 8d (2 marks) annually to provide meat and drink for their daughters until each reached the age of 15. If the age of majority was 16 why would John Hardwick have only provided for his daughters until their 15th birthday? Why not to their 16th? Bess's mother went on to marry Ralph Leche. Canon Law held that whereas a boy had to be 14 years of age to give his consent to marriage, girls could give consent from the age of 12. Boys under 14 and girls below the age of 12 were held to be too young to consummate the marriage.[10]

We know that around 1536 Ralph had purchased Robert Barley's wardship and marriage from Arthur Barley. If Bess was around 15 years of age at that time her mother would have ceased to receive the funds to provide for Bess's upkeep. Under such circumstances, it would have made perfect sense for Ralph to have been seeking to arrange Bess's marriage. It is probable that Bess and Robert Barley were espoused c1536 with the marriage ceremony and possible consummation of the marriage taking place later, that is prior to or shortly after Arthur Barley's death in 1543 when it could be argued that Robert had reached the age of consent for marriage. It is certainly possible that Bess may have moved into the Barley household after the espousal was agreed.

Applying modern notions of family life to the sixteenth-century family can lead to confusion and misinterpretation. It has been assumed that Bess was residing with her mother and stepfather at Hardwick before her marriage to

Robert Barley. However, Ralph seems to have been keen to avoid the expense of paying for the upkeep of his stepdaughters once the provisions in their father's will had lapsed. Before Jane Hardwick married Godfrey Boswell in the early to mid-1540s, she had been in service to a Lady Carew.

It is possible that on espousal both Bess and perhaps elder sister, Alice, may have gone to live in the household of their respective spouses. It appears that only Jane and Mary were residing at Hardwick in the early 1540s when they were visited there by John and Anne Wyke.[11] Assuming Jane was born in 1526/7 she would have reached the age of 15 in 1541/2 and it may have been around this time she entered Lady Carew's service, perhaps an arrangement brokered by Henry Marmion via his association with the Willoughbys. Absence of evidence, as one of my university professors used to say, is not evidence of absence.

There is no issue when it comes to the year John Hardwick's son James was born. As we have seen, James came out of wardship in 1546 so we can be certain that he was born in 1525. However, establishing the order of the births of John's daughters is more problematic. In a Chancery case begun c1546/7, Jane Hardwick's husband Godfrey Boswell listed John Hardwick's daughters as Mary, Elizabeth, Alice, Dorothy and Jane.[12] He was suing for an unpaid marriage portion and most likely named his wife last as she was the object of his proceedings.

The published version of the 1569 Herald's visitation of Derbyshire lists Hardwick's daughters as Jane, Mary, Elizabeth and Alice.[13] Dorothy, possibly born at some time between 1518 and 1521, is not mentioned in the visitations and probably died young. In an early written account, the daughters are listed as Alice, Elizabeth, Mary and Jane but in a 1615 copy of the 1569 visitation they are listed as Mary, Jane, Alice and Elizabeth. In the published version of the 1569 visitation, Alice and Mary are placed before their brother, James, but in two manuscript copies of the visitation Elizabeth and Jane are placed before James. Both hand-written pedigrees pair Alice with Elizabeth and Mary with Jane. Only the published version of the 1569 visitation pairs the daughters differently, but this appears to be the result of the layout of the printed page.

A manuscript pedigree dating from c1565 would appear to list John Hardwick's children in reverse order commencing with Mary (not actually named but described as the wife of Wingfield) followed by Jane, James, Elizabeth and 'Anna' (that is Alice)[14] Here again Mary is paired with Jane and Elizabeth with Alice. The most likely birth order of John Hardwick's daughters was Alice, Dorothy, Elizabeth, Jane and Mary. In the summer of 1540, Jane and Mary were the only two of Hardwick's daughters known to have been living at Hardwick.[15]

Ralph Leche married John Hardwick's widow around 1529. Alice, the eldest of John Hardwick's daughters, appears to have been the first to marry. Her ill-fated marriage to Francis Leche, her stepfather's nephew, may have been contracted sometime around her 15th birthday c1533, which incidentally would have coincided with John Bugby's eviction from Hardwick. Francis was born on 1 November 1525 and would not have reached the age of 14 until 1539. Bess is believed to have married Robert Barley in May 1543 but was espoused in 1536.

Jane, clearly younger than Bess, appears to have married Boswell in 1545/6. In each case, espousals would have been contracted well before the marriages took place. Mary was almost certainly the youngest of John Hardwick's daughters. Her marriage to Richard Wingfield appears to have been brokered by Sir William Cavendish and she was the only one of Hardwick's daughters not to marry into a local gentry family. Like Cavendish, the Wingfields were associated with Thomas Cromwell.

Although Bess had proved her fecundity during her marriage to Sir William Cavendish, it is possible that by the time of her marriage to Sir William St Loe, she was reaching the end of her child-bearing years. She would have been around 38 years of age at the time of the St Loe marriage and approaching her mid-40s at the time of St Loe's death. Women in the sixteenth century could have children well into their 30s. For example, Edward Seymour's second wife Anne Stanhope bore eleven children the last of which was born when she was 39/40. However, her first child was born when she was 16.

Bess was around 27 when her first child Frances was born in 1548 by which time her child-bearing years would have been well advanced. St Loe had no issue from his first marriage and did not remarry for some 10 years after his first wife's death. He cannot have been anxious to produce a male heir.[16] He and Bess spent much of their married life living apart: he in London, she at Chatsworth. There was no issue with the marriage.

The plaque on Bess's monument in Derby Cathedral states that she was around 87 when she died on 13 February 1608 indicating that 1521 was the year of her birth. Some object that the information on the plaque cannot be trusted because it refers to her grandson as 'Duke of Newcastle' which he did not become until 1655, 47 years after her death. However, all this shows is that a new plaque probably replaced an original one. The information regarding Bess's age at death given on the new plaque would simply have been copied from the original.

On his 52nd birthday, 20 November 1604, Gilbert Talbot wrote a letter to Robert Cecil in which he informed Cecil that Bess, his 'unkind mother-in-law', was then about 84 years of age. Had Bess moved into Hardwick New Hall on her 70th birthday, as has been claimed, Gilbert would surely have been aware of the fact and would therefore have thought her to have been around 77 in late 1604, not about 84. Clearly, members of her own family held that Bess was born in or around 1521, not 1527. This would seem to confirm that, as stated on the monument plaque, she would indeed have been some 87 years of age when she died in 1608.[17]

The Duchess of Newcastle stated that Robert Barley and Bess were both quite young at the time of their marriage and that despite having had 19 months in which to do so, Robert had died before the marriage had been consummated. However, she said this in 1667, over 120 years after the event and was simply attempting to make sense of what little was known at that time. According to law when a couple were espoused, unless coercion had been used, they were deemed to be married.[18] However, the marriage contract was not complete until the marriage ceremony had taken place and the marriage consummated. Bess and Robert may well have been quite young when they were espoused.

Espousals often involved two people whose ages were many years apart. It cannot be assumed that the marriage ceremony of Robert and Bess took place at the same time as the espousal. We do not know for certain when or where the marriage ceremony took place. Bess informed Chancery that both she and Robert were of 'tender years' when the marriage contract was agreed between Arthur Barley and Ralph Leche.[19] This suggests that the espousal was contracted sometime before any marriage ceremony took place.

It is possible that Robert and Bess's marriage ceremony took place shortly after Arthur Barley's death after Robert's removal from Barley Lees. The marriage is 'assumed' to have taken place shortly before the death of Arthur Barley on 28th May 1543 because when Godfrey Boswell purchased Robert's wardship from the crown a statement was added to the record stating that Robert was married in the lifetime of his father. To what extent this can be taken as reliable evidence of the timing of Bess's marriage to Robert is open to question. To limit the impact wardship would have on Arthur Barley's estate, it was in

Boswell's interest to have it recorded that Robert was married before his father died but what did Boswell mean by 'married'?

Today, marriage begins on the wedding day at the time the marriage ceremony takes place. In the sixteenth century, the mean age at first marriage for women in Bess's social rank was around 25.[20] The marriage process began at espousal but was not complete until the marriage ceremony had taken place and the marriage consummated. The act of consummation normally took place in front of witnesses within hours of the marriage ceremony. On the other hand, there could be many years between the spousal contract and the marriage ceremony.

Evidence suggests that the first stage of marriage, in this case the spousal contract for Robert's marriage to Bess, was agreed between Arthur Barley and Ralph Leche in the mid-1530s, clearly within the lifetime of Robert's father. Is this what Boswell meant by 'married', i.e., was he referring to the date of the spousal contract? We do not know if Robert's marriage to Bess was consummated, we do know that it produced no issue.

Matters of Death

The August 2018 edition of the BBC's *History* magazine included an article, 'Schemer, Social Climber… Scourge of Elizabeth I' written by a well-known celebrity historian in which, perhaps taking the cue from David Durant, the author informs readers that following her death in 1608 Bess's "body lay in great state at Hardwick until her funeral three months later."[21] I recall being told the same thing by a long time Hardwick room guide when I began my stint as a National Trust volunteer. Repeated *ad nausem*, it is utter nonsense!

It was long said that Mary, Queen of Scots, was at some time held in captivity at Hardwick. Of course, this myth has thankfully been consigned to the proverbial dustbin. However, many other myths persist. Bess did not meet her first husband in London and beyond speculation there is no hard evidence to show she was ever in service to the Zouches of Codnor or the Greys of Bradgate. It really does not help matters when 'celebrity historians' presenting material to the wider public on TV, radio, or in popular publications, repeat these myths and present them as facts.

Of course, we may not know that some of the things we say are myths. Make no mistake, myths are hard enough to dislodge even where the evidence we have screamed at us that something or other told time after time to visitors to such places as Hardwick are in fact myths. And the truth is that there are those among us, well-meaning souls no doubt, who are simply unwilling, or unable, to change their views even in the face of overwhelming evidence.

Let us now turn our attention to Bess's funeral. On 5 January 1608, Gilbert Talbot informed Robert Cecil that Bess's condition 'decayeth extremley.' A little over a month later she was dead. She died on 13 February 1608. Considering the bad relations between Bess and Mary Talbot, Gilbert told Cecil he was very surprised by the depth of distress displayed by his wife on hearing of her mother's death. But did Bess's body really lie in state in a lead coffin in Hardwick Hall's High Great Chamber for four months as has so often been said?

There are references in the Devonshire archives at Chatsworth House that indicate Bess's funeral took place on either the 16th or 17th of February together with an entry for February 1608 which states that the sum of £1 was distributed among the poor at the gates of Hardwick the day her corpse was transported to Derby.[22] In his unpublished 1692 manuscript *Lives of the Earls of Shrewsbury* Nathaniel Johnson included the following quote from a letter written by Sir John Bentley in 1608 dated the 18th February:

The Lord Cavendish, Mr William, his sister; myself, John Clay, John Needham, & all the women but Mrs. Digby, And Cartwright, & all the men of note but Pudsey, attended the Corps to Derby on Tuesday, Multitudes came in to behold our coming. The baylives stept with us, & presented wine & two suger loaves to his Lordshipp....[23]

We know that members of Bess's family stayed in two Derby inns at this time, The *George,* and *The Talbot.* Johnson's description fits well with Bess's own wishes for her funeral as expressed in her will. She asked to be buried without pomp and ceremony and typically without unnecessary expense.[24] Perhaps the definitive evidence in this case comes from Bess's contemporary Arthur Mower, who was a bailiff and collector for the Barleys. In February 1608, Mower wrote in his memorandum:

The old Countess of Shrewsbury departed forth of this world the Saturday being the 13th day of February at Hardwick and was carried to Derby of Tuesday the next after to her tomb there in All Hallows Church and there buried...[25]

In her 2018 *Devices & Desires*, author Kate Hubbard makes some effort to incorporate recent research but nevertheless repeats the myth that Bess's funeral took place in May 1608.[26] Bess's funeral took place on Tuesday, 16 February 1608. Her body did not lie in state at Hardwick for three months. So how did that myth come about? Records at Chatsworth refer to a funeral banquet or dinner held in May 1608.[27]

This funeral dinner was held in the more clement spring weather of May when travel would have been far easier than in the cold, frosty weather of a Derbyshire winter. The winter of 1607/8 saw the first recorded 'Frost Fair' on the River Thames. Misinterpreted as the date of Bess's funeral, it was the funeral dinner of May 1608 that gave rise to the myth that her corpse lay in state for three months in the High Great Chamber of Hardwick New Hall. The fact is it did not.

Gilbert Talbot's 1604 letter to Robert Cecil is the only contemporary evidence we have that specifically relates to Bess's year of birth. Parish registers were not introduced until 1538 and very few parishes have complete records from thence forward. There is no mention of a birthday in any of Bess's letters, sent or received. The weight of the evidence we have confirms that the year of Bess's birth was c1521 and that her funeral took place in Derby on Tuesday 16 February 1608.

References and Notes

[1] Devonshire MSS, Chatsworth, Hardwick MSS 7, Account Book of Countess of Shrewsbury, 1591-97, fol. 195; M. Girouard, *Robert Smythson and the Architecture of the Elizabethan Era*, London, 1966, 120. On page 3 of his 1977 Bess of Hardwick: *Portrait of an Elizabeth Dynast*, David Durant informs his readers that Bess was born in 1527. Mary Lovell in her *Bess of Hardwick: First Lady of Chatsworth*, page xiii, and elsewhere also opines that Bess was born in 1527. On page 55 of his *The Smythson Circle* first published in 2011 Durant says that Bess was "probably" born in 1527. On page 100 he shifts the word 'probably' to the place where Bess was born rather than the year, viz "Bess was born in 1527, probably at Hardwick." However, on page 158 of that volume Durant writes "…when Bess moved into her New Hardwick, she was eighty years old and her husband [George Talbot] had been dead for ten years." If Bess was 80 in October 1597 – the date she moved into the new hall – then she must have been some 90 years old when she died in February 1608. I doubt very much that Durant thought that to be the case. If we take the second part of Durant's statement – that George Talbot had been dead for ten years – that would bring us to 1600 as Talbot died in 1590. In this case, as stated on the plaque on her monument in Derby Cathedral, Bess would have been 87 when she died in February 1608 and therefore must have been born in or around 1521. Although Bess moved into the new hall in 1597 the building work was not completed until 1599/1600. The inventory of the finished and furnished new hall was undertaken in 1601. It is possible that Durant confused Canon Law with Common Law when discussing the ages of the majority.

[2] M. Barlow, *Barlow Family Records* (London) 1932, 23. Interestingly, the author indicates his belief that Bess was older than James, pedigree, p 143.

[3] A. Collins, *Historical Collections of the Noble Families of Cavendish, Holles, Vere, Harley and Ogle* (London: Printed for E. Withers, 1752), 18.

[4] In sixteenth-century law, the age of majority was 21 for males and females. A young female heiress who became subject to wardship was allowed to enter her inheritance at the age of 16 but this was not a universal female rite of passage. The first time the age of 16 took on any universal legal significance for woman came in

1929 when the Age of Marriage Act raised the age at which boys and girls could marry with the consent of a parent or guardian from 14 to 16. This remains the case today. Until 1753 a marriage ceremony Until 1753 a marriage ceremony could take place anywhere provided it was conducted by an ordained minister and independently witnessed. The custom was that consummation of a marriage took place after any reception often in the early hours of the morning and was witnessed by friends and relatives. The 1933 Children and Young Persons Act made it illegal for those under the age of 16 to buy tobacco and cigarettes. This was raised to 18 in 2015. Until 1970, the age at which men and women could vote was 21. Since 2003 codified laws allow those 18 and over to buy alcohol. However, harping back to the time when 21 was deemed the minimum age for buying alcohol many retailers ask for proof of age where customers look to be under 21 (or in some cases under 25). Even today, although it is legal for those over 18 to buy alcoholic drinks, many supermarket and off-licence chains display Challenge 21 (or Challenge 25) notices stating that they will not serve people who look to be under 21 (or 25) without ID. In the USA, most states still use 21 as the minimum legal age for the consumption of alcohol. Many more modern examples could be cited.

[5] TNA, C 1/1101/17. In his will, John Hardwick appointed Henry Marmion and John Leake as his children's guardians. Had Bess been under 21 when she commenced her legal proceedings for dower, she would then have been represented by either Marmion or Leake.

[6] TNA, C 1/1101/17; TNA, C 1/1120/44. For women and the law in the sixteenth century see A. Flower, Tudor Women's Legal Rights, 1485-1603 (2007).

[7] 'Pedigree of the Freschevile and Musard Families', Collectanea Topographica et Genealogica (1837), 4.

[8] P. Riden. 'The Hardwicks of Hardwick Hall in the Fifteenth and Sixteenth Centuries', Derbyshire Archaeological Journal, 130 (2010), 151.

[9] C 142/282/103.

[10] Flower, 23. Canon Law held that a marriage between a girl of 12 and a boy over 14 could be dissolved if it had not been consummated. Failure to consummate a marriage could and did result in child marriages being dissolved.

[11] TNA, STAC 2/17/53; TNA, STAC 2/22/240. See also chapter 6.

[12] TNA, C 1/1102/37-39.

[13] W.C. Metcalfe (ed), The Visitations of Derbyshire, 1569 and 1611, Vol 7, 1891, 142; Riden. 'The Hardwicks', 150.

[14] Belvoir Castle Muniments, box labelled 'pedigrees.'

[15] W.C. Metcalfe (ed), The Visitations of Derbyshire, 1569 and 1611, Vol 7, 1891; TNA, STAC 2/7, ff 15-16.

[16] See chapter 2.

[17] HMC, Cecil Papers, vol 16, p 360. Cecil Papers: November 1604, 16-30. https://www.british-history.ac.uk/cal-cecil-papers/vol116/pp 357-373

[18] In his Family, Sex and Marriage, Penguin, 1979, 30, Lawrence Stone writes "It cannot be emphasised too strongly that according to ecclesiastical law, the spousal was as legally binding a contract as the church wedding." See also, D. Cressy, Birth, Marriage & Death: Ritual, Religion, and the Life-Cycle in *Tudor and Stuart England*, OUP, Oxford, 1999, 316-332 passim.

[19] TNA, C 1/1101/17.

[20] For mean age at marriage see for example Cressy, 286, L. Stone, *The Crisis of the Aristocracy, 1558-1641*, OUP, 1979, 653-4. B Coward, *Social Change and Continuity in Early Modern England, 1550-1750*, Longman, Studies in History, London 1988, 20.

[21] T. Borman, 'Schemer, Social Climber… Scourge of Elizabeth I', *BBC History Magazine*, August 2018, 50 - 55. D. N. Durant, *Bess of Hardwick: Portrait of an Elizabethan Dynast*, p 223-224.

[22] Devonshire MSS, Chatsworth, Hardwick MS 29, 4.

[23] Nathaniel Johnson, *Lives of the Earls of Shrewsbury*, unpublished MS Chatsworth, 397-8.

[24] TNA, PROB 11/111/213.

[25] Woolley collection Brit Mus Add Mss 6671; 'The Memorandum of Arthur Mower', Barlow Family Records, Chapter 3, 24.

[26] Hubbard. K., *Devices & Desires: Bess of Hardwick and the Building of Elizabethan England* (London, Chatto & Windus), 2018, 296-97.

[27] Devonshire MSS., Chatsworth, Hardwick MS 29, 16.

6. The Marmion Connection

Arms of Marmion of Tamworth, Winteringham and Torrington

If students of Bess of Hardwick have come across any member of the Marmion family it will most likely have been Henry Marmion who, together with John Leake, was an executor of the last will and testament of Bess's father, John Hardwick. Although he features on numerous occasions in the Hardwick narrative, little is known about Henry and even less about his son Gabriel, grandson Francis and the thus far unidentified Marmion whom Bess's fourth husband, George Talbot, Earl of Shrewsbury, bore animosity towards describing him as his enemy and as Bess's 'right-hand man'.

The Marmions of Nottinghamshire were a cadet branch of an illustrious medieval family which can be traced from Robert son of Roger Marmion, who in the early twelfth century held lands in Lincolnshire and in Warwickshire near Tamworth (Staffs.).[1] The family is first found at Fontenay-le-Marmion (Calvados), about six miles south of Caen, in the mid-eleventh century. Robert died in 1144[2] and was succeeded by a son (d.c.1181), grandson (a prominent justice who died c1216-18)[3] and great-grandson of the same name. The last Robert died probably c1241-3. His son and heir, Philip, whose estates included the manor of Middleton (Warw.), later held by the Willoughbys, died in 1291, leaving three daughters and an illegitimate son.

The family's estates passed to William Marmion, the son and heir of Robert, the son of the justice. William appears to have been dead by 1276. His son and heir, Sir John Marmion, was summoned to Parliament between 1313 and 1322, thus becoming the 1st Lord Marmion. He died probably early in 1322, leaving a son and heir John, 2nd Lord Marmion, who is said to have died in 1335. His son and heir Robert was never summoned to Parliament and died without surviving male issue c1360 when the barony appears to have fallen into abeyance.

According to the nineteenth-century chronicler of the family, the Rippingale (Lincs.) branch of the Marmion family was descended from a younger son of the early thirteenth-century justice.[4] By the second half of the fifteen century, the Rippingale Marmions were headed by Henry Marmion's uncle, Mauncer Marmion (d 1506).

Henry Marmion was the eldest son and heir of another John Marmion (d. 1521). Alice, Henry's mother, was a daughter of Sir Hugh Willoughby (d. 1448).[5] John and Alice had another son named Francis and a daughter, Elizabeth. Possibly named for Sir Henry Willoughby (d. 1528), Henry Marmion was most likely born at Wollaton around 1495 and was a contemporary of Bess's father. On entering his inheritance in 1515/16, he commenced court proceedings to secure the repayment of a loan made by his father to Thomas Dixon, parson of Rippingale (S Lincs).[6]

In April 1545, Henry appointed John Burton as his attorney in a legal case in Bourne, also in south Lincolnshire, in relation to the surrender to George Machell, a relative of the Marmions, of a property formerly belonging to the monastery at Bourne.[7] At some date before 1547 Marmion was among several men accused of forcibly resisting an attempted arrest of Machell at Rippingale.[8] Among the defendants were Edith Marmion (d. 1538) of Lincolnshire, widow, and her son Edward. Edith was the daughter of Sir Thomas Berkley of Wymondham, Norfolk,[9] and the wife of Mauncer Marmion. They had three sons, Edward, William and Thomas, and a daughter, Petronell, who together with Henry Marmion was an executrix of her mother's will of 1539.[10]

Edward went on to become the parson of St Botolph's, Billingsgate, in London. In his will, dated 23 September 1540,[11] he referred to his sister Petronell and to his cousin Henry Marmion's two daughters, Bridget and Ursula. Mauncer held the family estates, which suggests that Henry's father, John, was a younger brother. Mauncer's will, dated 8 November 1505, tells us that their father was another John Marmion and that their Lincolnshire ancestors were laid to rest in St Anne's chapel in the church of St Andrew at Rippingale.[12] The executors of Mauncer's will were his wife Edith and Sir Henry Willoughby.

In January 1519, John Willoughby and John Marmion presented Thomas Marmion (d. 1529/30)[13] as the new rector of the parish church of Dowesby (Lincs.)[14] William Marmion (d. 1520/1)[15] married Alice, the widow of John Marsden, and died sometime between 1515 and 1518. Alice was evicted from the farm she and William had shared at Ringsdon (Lincs). She commenced proceedings in Chancery against the two executors of William's will, his mother Edith and his brother Edward. Alice revived these proceedings after Edith's death in 1538. On this occasion, the defendants were Petronell and Henry Marmion.[16] Katherine, William Marmion's heir, became a king's ward. She married John Haslewood (d. 1550) of Maidwell. Northamptonshire, who was master of the Fleet prison between 1548 and 50.[17] They commenced proceedings in Chancery against her grandmother Edith and her uncle Edward in relation to several manors in Lincolnshire and Leicestershire, which were part of her late grandfather Mauncer Marmion's estate.[18] In April 1535, a writ of Oyer and Terminer was issued by the Kesteven JP Thomas Gildon relating to an alleged assault on Haselwood by Henry Marmion.[19] It was probably during this affray that the attempt to arrest Machell had been made. Haselwood and his wife brought further complaints before Star Chamber alleging that Katherine had not received her dower or dues from her father's estate. Among the defendants were Edith, Edward, Machell and Henry Marmion.[20]

In June 1508, John Marmion was an executor of the will of Sir Henry Willoughby. By 30 October 1509, a marriage had been agreed between John Marmion and John Malory of Walton on the Wolds in Leicestershire in which Henry was to marry Malory's daughter Margaret.[21] As part of this agreement, Margaret's marriage portion of land and tenements to an annual value of £10 at Walton and Croxton, also in Leicestershire, were enfeoffed to the use of Henry and Margaret and their heirs. The feoffees were Sir Henry Willoughby, Sir Ralph Shirley, Sir John Digby, John Willoughby, William Wymesold, and Robert Peret (or Perrot), chaplain of Wollaton. The marriage settlement illustrates how such arrangements were business transactions.

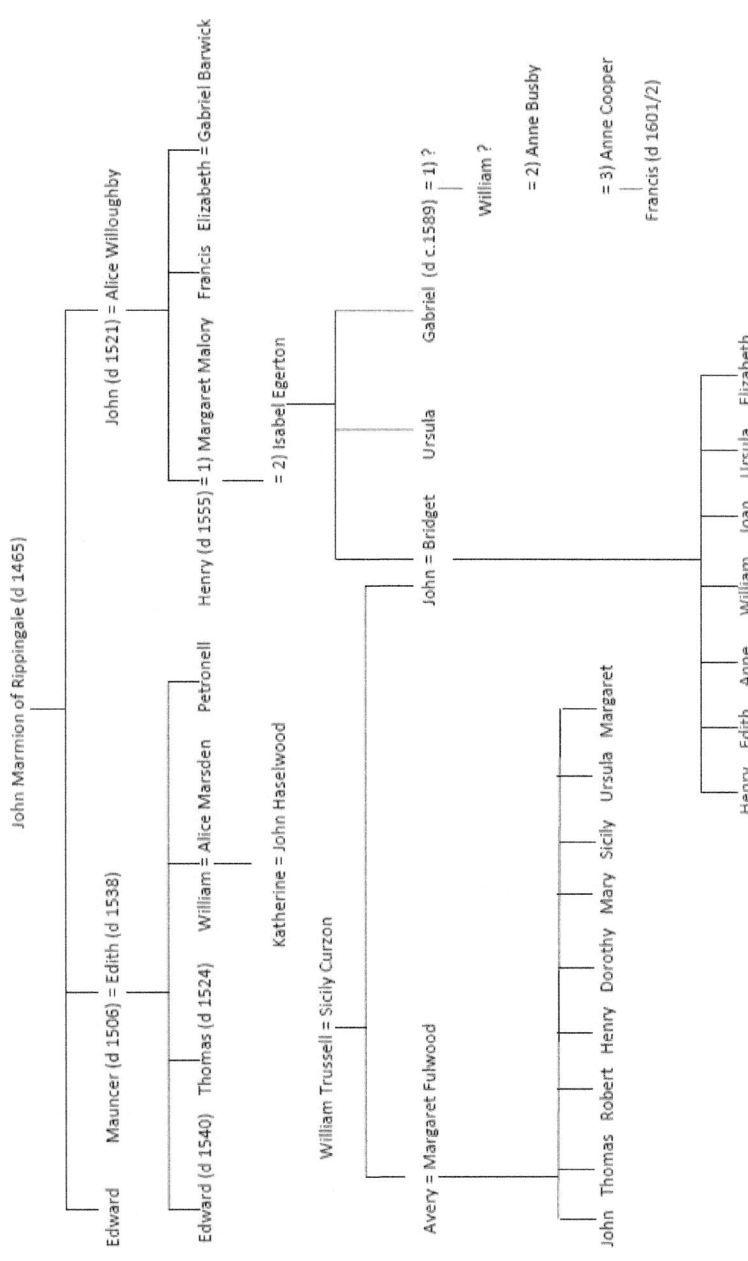

Marmion Pedigree

105

If Henry were to die before the marriage was consummated Margaret was to marry his brother Francis. Should Margaret die first Henry, on the advice of his father, was to marry another of John Malory's daughters. Should any of the marriages prove childless the marriage portion was to pass to John Malory's heirs. In February 1546, the lands and tenements at Croxton and Walton were transferred to Henry and Margaret under the Statute of Uses. Henry also received further bequests of a bay colt and 40s from his father's will.[22]

There were long-standing connections between the gentry families of north-east Derbyshire and the Willoughbys of Wollaton and Middleton. Sir Hugh Willoughby (d. 1448) married Isabel Foljambe of Walton near Chesterfield. Their son Richard (d. 1471) married Anne Leake of Cotham and their grandson, Sir Henry (d. 1528) took as his first wife Robert Markham's daughter, Margaret (d. 1490). They were the parents of John, Edward, another Henry and several daughters.[23]

In 1496, one of these daughters, Margaret Willoughby, married Sir John Zouche of Codnor. They were the parents of Sir George Zouche, who married Anne Gainsford. In 1500, Henry Willoughby was among a group of feoffees appointed by Sir John Zouche to hold Codnor and his other Derbyshire estates.[24] One of the executors of the will of Henry, Lord Grey of Codnor (d. 1525), was Bess's maternal grandfather Thomas Leake who, together with Roger Johnson, was seised of the manor and castle of Codnor at the time of Lord Grey's death.[25] Grey had promised to sell Codnor to the Crown, which then sold the estate to Sir John Zouche.

John Leake, Bess's great-uncle, can also be linked to the Zouches and Codnor Castle. In the early 1540s, Sir George Zouche and his wife took seisin of Codnor Castle. Edward Willoughby married Anne, the daughter of Sir William Filliol of Woodlands, Dorset, whose sister Catherine (d. 1535) was married to Edward Seymour, the Lord Protector, and was the mother of John and Edward Seymour. They remained loyal to their father despite being disinherited by him. Edward spent part of 1551 in the Tower of London and his brother John died a prisoner there in 1552.[26]

In 1489, 1495 and 1507, Sir Henry Willoughby was among the feoffees chosen by members of the Hardwick family to hold lands on their behalf.[27] In 1528 Bess's father made his will and enfeoffed his estate to Sir Henry Willoughby's son Edward, John Leake, Thomas Leake, Edward Beresford, Richard Spalton, Robert Peret and Henry Marmion.[28] Henry was a servant of the Willoughbys. Like his father he was a bailiff and collector.[29] We know that at one stage he lived at Aspley Hall in Radford (Notts.),[30] a property held by Lenton priory until it passed to the Willoughbys after the dissolution of the monastic houses. It was Sir Francis Willoughby's temporary home during the building of Wollaton Hall. In 1536, Henry acquired a twenty-year lease of a cottage and land at Basford (Notts.) from Hugh Willoughby of Maxstoke, Warwickshire. [31] In July 1544 Henry leased a messuage he was occupying in Cossall from Sir John Willoughby for 21 years at an annual rent of 40s. 10d.[32] In February 1523 Sir Henry Willoughby paid Henry Marmion 20s. In relation to correspondence and money sent to Edward Willoughby in London and in November, an unnamed servant of Marmion was paid 1s. for the delivery of a letter.[33]

Sir Henry died in 1528, and we learn from his will that Marmion had become one of two bailiffs of Wollaton Park. His duties included the 'keepershipe and payling and reconyng of Coles',[34] i.e. he had responsibility for maintaining the park pale and assessing royalties on coal. Several accounts in the Willoughby papers refer to Henry as bailiff of coal pits at Wollaton, Middleton, Sutton Passeys, Gedling, Carlton, Trowell, Cossall and elsewhere including pits in Warwickshire and Leicestershire.[35] Those for 1544-5 inform us that Henry's annual fee was £5, making him one of the Willoughbys's highest paid servants.[36]

In July 1544, just five months before the death of Bess's first husband, Sir John Willoughby appointed Henry Marmion keeper of Wollaton Park for life with an annual fee of £5, a gated pasture within the park for a horse or five cows, and the right to collect wood and windfall. Henry's fee was to be paid from the profits of Cossall and all Sir John's other manors in Nottinghamshire, excluding Wollaton. Should the fee not be paid for any reason Henry was entitled to distrain goods from those lands. At his own cost, he was to provide good quality timber for repairing the park pale. [37] In September 1545, Henry's tenure of the keepership of Wollaton park was confirmed by Sir Henry Willoughby.[38]

On 1 March 1548, Henry sold a capital messuage known as Le Ram situated in High Pavement,[39] Nottingham, which comprised a garden, outbuildings and taverns above and below ground to Joanna Hampton, her heirs and assigns. Sir Henry's will of 1549 referred to Henry as his 'trusty servant'.[40] Like Willoughby's other servants Marmion was often on the move, travelling from Wollaton to the sites of other Willoughby coalpits, as well as occasional journeys further afield to Bradgate, near Leicester, London and elsewhere.[41]

Sir Edward and Anne Filliol were the parents of another Sir Henry Willoughby, who inherited the estates of Wollaton and Middleton in January 1549 but was killed in Norfolk suppressing the Kett Rebellion in August that year.[42] His wife was Anne Grey (d. 1548), daughter of Thomas Grey, Marquis of Dorset, and sister of Henry Grey of Bradgate. Sir Henry Willoughby's untimely death in the summer of 1549 led to his young sons, Thomas and Francis, and their sister Margaret, first cousins to Henry Grey's daughters Jane, Katherine and Mary, being placed in wardship, initially with their uncle at Bradgate. Shortly afterwards Francis and Margaret became the wards of another uncle, George Medley (d. 1562/3) of Titley, Essex, half-brother of Anne Willoughby and brother-in-law of both Henry Grey and Sir Henry Willoughby. As one of Sir Henry's 'three trusty servants', Medley joined Henry Marmion and Gabriel Barwick as witnesses of Sir Henry's will.

As guardians of Sir Henry's children, they blocked a proposed marriage between Francis and Sir Francis Knollys's daughter, Elizabeth.[43] Medley had a house at the Minories in London, roughly midway between Aldgate and the Tower of London, where they were visited by Lady Grey and her daughters. Medley was placed in the Tower in the wake of the Jane Grey affair and again at the time of the Wyatt rebellion when the Minories were searched for incriminating evidence. Thereafter, Lady Grey met the costs of Francis's upkeep and education whilst Margaret was moved back to Bradgate. Thomas Willoughby had initially remained at Bradgate but was moved to London where he became the ward of Sir William Paget and married Dorothy, one of Paget's daughters.

Thomas died in 1559, leaving his younger brother Francis as heir to the Wollaton and Middleton estates, of which he entered into possession in 1564.[44] There is ample evidence to show that the Greys, the Willoughbys and servants of both families regularly travelled between Wollaton and Bradgate.[45] Bess was always on good terms with Sir Francis Willoughby and several of her letters to him survive.[46] She paid visits to Wollaton and provided substantial loans and mortgages for Sir Francis's use. She also made good use of Sir Francis's servants, including his surveyor, Robert Smythson, the architect of Hardwick New Hall, and his master masons John and Christopher Rhodes. Thomas Accres, who had worked for Bess before being employed at Wollaton, returned to her employment in August 1594.[47]

According to a 1545/6 legal action taken by her husband Godfrey Boswell, John Hardwick's daughter Jane was at some point 'in the service of Lady Carowe, wife of Sir George Carowe, knight'.[48] The Carews were among those West Country families who became part of the Grey affinity. As captain of the ill-fated *Mary Rose*, Sir George went to his death on 19 July 1545. Some members of the Carew family supported Jane Grey and, along with Henry Grey, George's brother, Sir Peter Carew, was one of the principals of the Wyatt Rebellion. It is possible that Jane Hardwick's service with the Carews may have stemmed from this connection.

We know that Jane and her sister Mary were residents at Hardwick in August 1540. Their mother was probably living at Hardwick. Bess may well have been living with the Barleys. Boswell's legal action refers to a period when 'as such time as Jane was' in service to Lady Carew the wife of Sir George Carew but does not say exactly when this was. However, he does not describe Lady Carew as a widow and therefore Jane must have been in Lady Carew's service before July 1545.

In the autumn of 1540, Sir George married his second wife, Mary, daughter of Sir Henry Norris.[49] It may be that Jane entered her service around that time and left before July 1545, possibly in 1542 when aged 23 Godfrey Boswell entered into his inheritance, the same year that Jane would have reached the age of 15 and the funding provided for her upkeep in her father's will would have ceased.

Clear links can be demonstrated between the Willoughbys of Wollaton, the Zouches of Codnor, the Greys of Bradgate and numerous others among which were the Hardwicks. It seems probable that Henry Marmion and John Hardwick knew each other before Henry was named a feoffee in 1528. Hardwick named Francis Talbot, 5th Earl of Shrewsbury, and Sir John Savage as supervisors of his will and John Leake (d. 1545) and Henry Marmion as executors. Leake was his wife's uncle and the Leakes were also related to the Savages by marriage. Like his father, John Hardwick held land of both the Savage and Leake families.[50]

The choice of Marmion may have been the result of Willoughby's influence but may also indicate that a good degree of trust already existed between John Hardwick and Henry Marmion. John gave custody of his daughters to his wife until they reached the age of 15. Each daughter was left a marriage portion of 40 marks (£26 6s. 8d.) and was to adhere to the counsel of his executors.[51] Marmion and John Leake were to be the guardians of Hardwick's children.

John Hardwick's only son and heir James was within age at the time of his father's death and therefore subject to wardship. In March 1530, the Court of Wards sold James's wardship for £20 to a courtier named John Bugby. Probably with a degree of exaggeration conventional in Star Chamber proceedings, in 1533 Bugby claimed to have been forcibly evicted from Hardwick Hall by a gang of men led by John Leake and Henry Marmion.[52] According to Bugby's complaint, Marmion, Leake, Robert Garard, Jasper Flower and others, including a widow named Elizabeth Williamson, attacked Hardwick Hall 'riotously and with force', smashed glass in the windows, broke into the house and threw Bugby out. The widow's role would presumably have been to bring succour and comfort to Elizabeth and her children living in the house at the time. Bugby referred to several 'high commandments under great penalties' that had been sent to those accused but which had been ignored and therefore asked that the accused be ordered to appear before Star Chamber.

Bugby's allegations were answered by Marmion and Leake who, aware that the penalties for riotous behaviour were severe, denied the accusations that any riot had occurred or that force had been used. They argued that Bugby's allegations were false and that the evidence against them was insufficient. They requested that the case be transferred from Star Chamber to the common law courts, probably because they knew that local jurors were sufficiently in their pocket that they would find in their favour, regardless of the truth of the matter. Also, if the case was to go to a common law court, the verdict would be a simple win or lose, based on a far more rigid interpretation of the law than might be possible under equity in Star Chamber, and they presumably saw that as helpful to them.

Around 1540, Marmion was alleged to have organised an attack on Chatsworth for which he, Bess's mother and others were brought before the Derby assizes and were later investigated by Star Chamber.[53] John Wykes claimed that Roger Leche had enfeoffed lands at Chatsworth to the use of his wife Anne for her lifetime, with reversion to Roger's son Francis Leche after Anne's death. Wykes married Anne in 1536. Wykes alleged that around 6 o'clock on the morning of 2 August 1540, Henry Marmion, his servant Nicholas Waterhouse, Edmund Plattes, who was Jane Hardwick's servant, and John Wild, of Hardwick, yeoman, together with a dozen or more 'evil-disposed and riotous persons', launched an armed attack on Langley Close at Chatsworth, assaulted Anne Wykes and Mary Hone, and then drove off with three cartloads of wheat sheaves. When questioned by Star Chamber, Wild, Waterhouse and Plattes all denied charges of riotous or unlawful assembly, forcible entry, assault or battery and asked that the case be tried at common law.

The defendants also claimed that after Roger Leche died, Anne held the property for her life and married a George Findern and that they leased Langley Close to Henry Marmion. Henry manured the land and sowed it with wheat. Before the wheat was ripe, Findern died, and Anne married John Wykes. Meanwhile, Henry Marmion sold the crops growing in Langley Close to Jane and Mary Hardwick. At harvest time, Jane and Mary ordered John Wild and Edmund Plattes to cut the crops and Marmion instructed Waterhouse to deliver them to Hardwick which, they stated, they did in a peaceful manner.

Wykes claimed that during the attack his wife's head was 'broken' and that one of the defendants left behind a wood knife and other weapons. According to Wild, Henry Marmion, Elizabeth Leche, Edmund Plattes, Nicholas Waterhouse, Robert Simpson, Thomas Thorpe and Wild himself were indicted and brought before the justices at Derby. There the defendants repeated their claim that they had not behaved in a riotous manner and stated that as Marmion's lease to Langley Close had been granted by Findern it became void on his death. Realising this, Marmion had granted the crops growing on the land to Jane and Mary Hardwick, pretending it to be a sale. The defendants also claimed that Wykes and Anne went to see Jane and Mary and offered to allow the crops to be taken on condition that the sisters acknowledged Anne Wyke's rights over the land.

The two sisters refused and arranged for the defendants to carry away the crops. Although Bess's mother was mentioned, no mention was made of Bess and it is possible she was then living with the Barleys. Waterhouse accepted that the knife was his but denied that it had been used for any violent purposes or that Anne Wykes's head had been 'broken'. They also denied that Henry Marmion had unlawfully granted the crops to the Hardwicks. Wild stated that several women armed with pikes and staves had attacked the defendants as they took away the crops.

He admitted that he had hit Anne Wykes and Mary Hone with his gadd (a sharp, pointed stick) and stated that he was responsible for having 'broken' Anne Wykes's head but he only did so in self-defence. The defendants agreed that they had been paid for their services by Henry Marmion and Jane and Mary Hardwick. Jane and Mary were not indicted.

Bess's stepfather Ralph Leche purchased the marriage and wardship of Robert Barley in the 1530s. No later than 1538, when Ralph was in the Fleet prison for debt and accused of desertion by Bess's mother, Henry Marmion claimed that he had purchased Robert's marriage and wardship from Ralph.[54] John Hardwick's will of 1528 provided money for his daughters' maintenance until they reached the age of 15. In Bess's case, this meant that she would have been provided for by her father's will until 1536/7, which tallies with the period during which Ralph Leche probably purchased Robert Barley's wardship and marriage. In 1543/4, Peter Freschevile of Staveley began proceedings against Ralph, Bess's mother and Henry Marmion, alleging that they had forcibly abducted Robert Barley and that a supposed marriage at an unspecified date between Robert and Bess was illegal.[55]

At the same time, Robert Barley's mother commenced proceedings for dower in the Barley estate and Henry Marmion was again one the defendants.[56] In Bess's 1546 proceedings for dower in Chancery against George Barley and his guardian Peter Freschevile, she stated that large sums of money had been paid for Robert's marriage and wardship by an unspecified number of friends but did not say who these were or how much was paid.[57] She may have been referring to Ralph Leche's initial payment to Arthur Barley, Robert's father, the payment of £41. 9s. 2d that Henry Marmion claimed to have paid to Ralph,[58] and the 100 marks paid by Godfrey Boswell to the Court of Wards.[59]

Boswell married Bess's sister, Jane Hardwick, in or just before 1545/6, which may indicate that Jane was younger than Bess. We know that Ralph Leche was then in the Fleet prison 'condemned in great sums of money'.[60] It was also at that time that Sir James Foljambe began legal proceedings against Ralph Leche 'late of London', Bess's mother Elizabeth Leche of Hardwick Hall, Godfrey Boswell and Joan his wife late of Hardwick Hall, and their servant Edmund Plattes, to recover a debt of 20 marks.[61] Henry Marmion was not involved in this case but in 1545/6 Boswell commenced a suit in Chancery against him and John Leake (and again in 1546/7 against John's son and heir, Francis) with respect to unpaid money owed to his wife.[62]

Boswell claimed that Marmion, Leake and Ralph Leche had embezzled hundreds of pounds which, as John Hardwick's executors, Marmion and Leake should have paid to Hardwick's daughters. Boswell stated that when Jane had been in the service of Lady Carew, Marmion had given £15 for Jane's apparel to her mother but that nothing else had been paid to any of John Hardwick's daughters.[63] Apart from this payment of £15, we know nothing of Jane Hardwick's service with Lady Carew.

Having secured her marriage to Godfrey Boswell it seems doubtful that a debt-ridden Ralph Leche would have wanted the financial burden of welcoming a 23-year-old newly widowed Bess back into the family after less than two years of marriage to Robert Barley. Bess was left to battle in the courts for her widow's dower and at one point in 1545 offered to settle the matter in return for her £26. 6s. 8d. marriage portion. It has often been claimed that around this time Bess entered the service of the Greys or the Zouches[64] but nothing is known of how such an arrangement might have come about. The Willoughbys were related to both the Greys and the Zouches. We have already seen that there is clear evidence linking the Leakes with the Zouches and it is possible that Bess may have been recommended to the Zouches by the Leakes.

Henry Marmion was a valued and trusted servant of the Willoughbys and the evidence we have demonstrates that Marmion did have a care for John Hardwick's children and generally adhered to the commitments placed on him by John's will. In December 1554, during a dispute between the Leakes and the Linacres, George Barley and three others, including Henry Marmion, were commissioned by Star Chamber to take depositions. Henry appears to have played no active role in the proceedings and died shortly before the hearing was held in Chesterfield on 17 January 1555.[65]

Henry Marmion died at Wollaton in January 1555 having been predeceased by his first wife Margaret Malory. In August 1564, an inquest was held at Lutterworth, Leicestershire, to enquire into the lands and tenements in Croxton and Walton which Henry had received from Margaret's father John Malory at the time of the marriage.[66] The jury stated that Henry had died without 'heirs of his and Margaret's bodies'. In November 1522, accounts refer to a payment of 6s. 8d. made by Sir Henry Willoughby to Gabriel Barwick, who is described as the husband of Henry Marmion's sister Elizabeth.[67] In 1525, a half-year wage of the 20s each was paid to Henry Marmion and Barwick.[68]

In June of that year, Henry was one of three men chosen by Sir Henry Willoughby to act as feoffees in relation to a messuage and lands in Bramcote belonging to Hugh Wright.[69] Three years later Gabriel, George Medley and John Hall were the executors of Sir Henry Willoughby's will.[70] In 1539, Barwick was appointed a co-feoffee by Arthur Barley in his efforts to minimise the impact of wardship on the Barley estate. Marmion, Barwick, and his servant were paid dinner expenses in 1542 when they attended Nottingham assizes. Henry was paid his fee of £5 in 1546 whilst Gabriel received 53s. 4d.[71]

In his will of 1548, Sir John Willoughby granted Gabriel an annuity of 26s. He also bequeathed £20 each to his sister Alice Draycott and her daughter, another Alice, with the proviso that should either or both die before the legacy was paid, the money of the deceased was to go to Henry Marmion and Barwick. Also mentioned in the will was a sum of £3 3 s. which Marmion and Barwick were to hold jointly for a period of twenty years; £3 was to be dispersed among the poor and the remaining 3 s. was to go to the residents of Willoughby's two Wollaton alms-houses. The rents of lands in Wigginton, near Tamworth, with a yearly value of 26s. 8d., were granted to Henry and Gabriel for twenty years, the income to be used to repair roads and bridges and at their discretion for any other charitable deeds.[72]

Sir John named Barwick as an executor of his will and Henry Marmion was among the witnesses. Together with John Hall, Gabriel from time to time presided over the Willoughby's court baron at Cossall.[73] Gabriel Barwick made his will in February 1568 and left 40s. to his godson, Gabriel Marmion. Barwick died in 1570.[74]

Willoughby family papers refer to Gabriel Marmion as having been among Sir Francis Willoughby's favourite servants.[75] Henry Marmion's inquisition states that his marriage to Margaret Malory was childless.[76] The 1569 heralds' visitation of Nottinghamshire indicates that Henry married again after Margaret's death.[77] His second wife was Isabel, daughter of John Egerton of Wrinehill, Staffordshire (d. 1529). Sir Henry Willoughby's third wife was Helen, Egerton's eldest daughter. Henry Marmion was, therefore, Sir Francis's brother-in-law.[78]

As we have seen, Edward Marmion's will states that Henry had two daughters, Bridget and Ursula. The 1569 visitation lists Bridget, daughter of Henry Marmion, as the wife of John Trussell gent. of Cossall and informs us that the couple named one of their daughters Ursula.[79] Trussell came from a Warwickshire family and by the early 1540s was in service with the Willoughbys at Wollaton. Like Henry Marmion, he was a bailiff and collector and the two men are frequently paired together in the Willoughbys' accounts.[80] In 1568 Gabriel Barwick chose Trussell as an executor of his will.[81]

Although Edward Marmion's will refers only to Henry Marmion's daughters it does not mean that Henry did not have a son (or sons) who may have been provided for outside the will or, more likely, born after 1540.[82] Gabriel Marmion was almost certainly Henry's son, probably named for Gabriel Barwick. He emerges in the historical record in 1568 among the beneficiaries of Barwick's will and the following year he was one of the parties in a deed of sale.[83] In 1576, described as Bess's servant, Gabriel had the important job of being one of the witnesses to Bess and the Earl of Shrewsbury's settlement relating to the estate of Sir William Cavendish.[84] In a letter to Bess dated 21 June 1580 the earl asked her to arrange for 'Marmyon' to meet his son Gilbert at Bakewell but did not give this man's Christian name.[85]

In a letter dated 24 October (the year is not given) to Sir Francis Willoughby the writer, 'Marmyon', described himself as a man the Earl of Shrewsbury could not abide but again did not give his Christian name. He informed Sir Francis that he and Bess were blamed by Shrewsbury for the earl's loss of favour with Queen Elizabeth, of having spoken egregiously against him and of having been responsible for the queen's reduction in the allowance received by the earl for the Queen of Scots' diet. The writer also said that he knew he was hated by the earl on the grounds that he was his bitter enemy and Bess's 'right-hand man'.[86] The allowance the earl received for the Scottish queen's diet was reduced on 29 January 1581 and she was removed from Shrewsbury's custody in August 1584. By 1583, Shrewsbury and Bess were no longer living as husband and wife and in July 1584 she was forced to leave Chatsworth.[87]

The writer of the letter to Sir Francis stated that he had been reluctant to leave Sir Francis Willoughby's household to serve Bess and was anxious to return saying 'Wollaton House should not be without a Marmyon', possibly a reference to the fact that the writer was aware that Gabriel Marmion was preparing to leave Wollaton. The identity of the writer is uncertain. From the 1550s entries in the Willoughby papers tend to refer to 'Marmyon' but, as with Shrewsbury's 1580 letter to Bess, the entries fail to provide a Christian name. It has been suggested that the writer was the William Marmion mentioned in the Willoughby accounts for 1572.[88] However, according to a Chancery deposition of 1602,[89] Gabriel had only one child, Francis, born c1586, who was probably named for Sir Francis Willoughby.

The fact that the writer mentions his father would seem to rule out William as having been the author. When he left her employ Bess provided the writer with

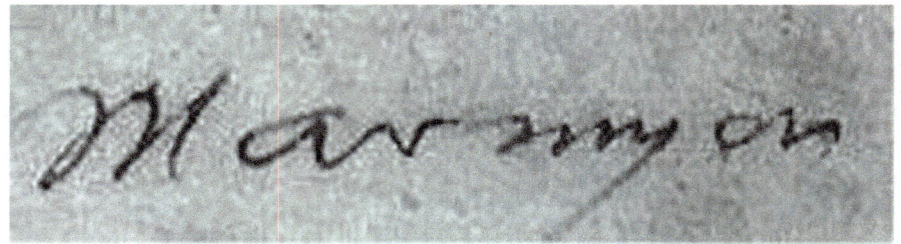

"…Wollaton house should not be without a Marmyon", 1582/3

'Marmyon', letter-writer, 1582/3

Gabriel Marmion, indenture signature, 1576

Gabriel Marmion, indenture signature, 1584

an annuity of £40 which was to be paid out of the lands of her son William Cavendish. This encouraged him to hope that his unnamed father-in-law would be assured that he was able to support his wife, which in turn suggests that she may still have been living with her father.

The 1582/3 letter to Sir Francis Willoughby does not appear to have been written by Gabriel. The handwriting of the 1582/3 letter-writer appears to be different to that of Gabriel Marmion. The letter-writer's hand shows a distinct left to right upward-sloping character. There are also clear differences in the formation of the capital letter 'M' and lowercase letters 'r', 'y', and 'n'.

Gabriel appears to have written in an early to mid-sixteenth-century secretarial hand whereas the letter-writer wrote in a more 'modern' hand which suggests he was a younger man. However, the letter contains a significant clue indicating that the writer was the son of Gabriel when he writes that Bess was supporting his father's 'cause against Browne'.[90] The will of Thomas Busby of Mayfield, Staffordshire, refers to Gabriel Marmion as the testator's son-in-law.[91] It does not name Gabriel's wife, who is not mentioned in the will and may not have been alive when it was written. However, in 1602 she is identified as Anne Haste alias Harryson alias Busby',[92] Thomas Busby's 'base daughter'.

Had she had two other husbands before Gabriel, or, far more likely, one or both, of the other surnames refers to her mother (who may have been born Haste and married a Harrison, or vice-versa). The 'alias Busby' presumably indicates that Thomas Busby acknowledged her as his daughter. The fact that she is not described as 'alias Marmion' is probably to avoid confusion with the defendant, but it is also possible that the will was drawn up after their betrothal and that Anne had died before or soon after marriage to Gabriel. Thomas Busby's will may have been designed to reward Gabriel for marrying his illegitimate (but by 1577 deceased) daughter, or they were still married or about to be married. However, the will refers consistently to the 'heirs of Gabriel' pointedly not to Gabriel and Busby's daughter, which is unusual.

Either this was a very deliberate sop to Gabriel, allowing his family to keep the money even if Anne died, or Anne had already died. Busby's wife Isabel was to enjoy the issues, revenues and profits of her husband's lands and farms in Mayfield and Burston in the manor of Stone, Staffordshire. These were to pass to Gabriel or his heir male on condition that within two months of Isabel's death, he bound himself to pay £5 twice yearly to Busby's daughter Agnes, alias Harrison. Either the will was reflecting an unusually advantageous arrangement for Gabriel—something that a father would not normally have proposed for a legitimate daughter—possibly to induce him to marry an illegitimate daughter, or Anne Busby was dead when Busby made his will and Gabriel was being compensated for his loss. Should Gabriel die without a male heir this part of Isabel's legacy was to pass to William Browne, Mary his wife and their heirs male. Mary Browne was Isabel's daughter but is nowhere described as a daughter of Thomas Busby.

Busby's will was not proved until 1584, seven years after his death, and possibly due to the birth of Gabriel's son Francis in 1585/6 the dispute between Gabriel and Browne seems to have abated. It was to re-emerge after Gabriel's death when the date of his death and that of Francis appear to have been a central issue. Anne Busby may not have been Gabriel's first wife. William Marmion may have been Gabriel's son from an earlier marriage and died before his father.

Gabriel's marriage to Anne Cooper could have been prompted by Gabriel's need for a male heir. Gabriel died intestate sometime between 1587 and 1589. In January 1590, Gabriel's widow Anne applied for a grant to administer her late husband's estate [93] and on 18 April 1594 Sir Francis Willoughby granted her a licence to alienate property in Arnold.[94] In April the following year she was conveyed a cottage and land in nearby Basford.[95]

In 1602, William Browne commenced proceedings in Chancery against Anne Marmion.[96] A writ dated 28 June 1602 called for depositions to be taken and these were presented to the court on 9 October. They provide a good deal of additional information which helps to clarify Brown's continuing grievances. Gabriel's wife Anne Cooper had provided him with a male heir, Francis, who died of smallpox in 1601/2 at the age of 16 years 10 months. According to the deposition made by Ralph Smith, Anne made Francis make a will leaving the income from the Busby lands and farms to her.

Busby's will refers to another daughter, Agnes Busby alias Harrison. Rowland Harrison of Hassop, Derbyshire, probably a relative of Anne and Agnes Busby, stated in his deposition that Francis had made him sole executor of his will but he had refused and so administration was granted to Anne Marmion. This was confirmed by others including Anne's son Robert Cooper and Henry Watts of Aston near Stone (Staffs.) who had married Isabel Busby. Busby's will intended that, for the remaining term of his leases, the profits of his lands and farms in Mayfield and Burston were to go to his wife Isabel during her lifetime.

After her death, they were to pass to Gabriel and his heir male or, should that line die out, to William and Mary Browne. Isabel outlived Mary Browne, Gabriel and his son Francis but she herself was dead by June 1602. Anne Marmion had retained the profits from the Staffordshire lands and farms. By the terms of Busby's will, Francis should not have been able to grant the profits accruing from the lands and farms to his mother, even if his mother had been Busby's daughter.

A brief note to Sir Francis Willoughby dated 28 October was added to the margin of the letter of 24 October in which the writer refers to having his own male servant. The writer must have travelled from Chatsworth to Sheffield between the 24 and 28 October when the letter was sent. Given Shrewsbury's animosity towards the writer, the fact that the letter, with the addition, was sent from Sheffield suggests that it was written before Bess was driven out of Chatsworth in July 1584. In other words, in October 1582 or 1583. Although there seems to be no firm evidence that William Marmion was a son of Gabriel it remains a possibility as the depositions of 1602 stating that Francis was Gabriel's only child may relate to a child then living or solely born to Anne Cooper and need not be conclusive evidence that Gabriel did not have a son with another wife.

William may have been Gabriel's son and left Wollaton in 1572 to enter Bess's service. He may also have been the Marmion referred to in Shrewsbury's letter of 1580. It is possible that William was the writer of the letter of 24 October. The letter was presumably despatched on or shortly after the addition was penned, i.e. 28 October 1582 or 1583. On leaving Bess's service, the writer, armed with his £40 annuity, expressed a desire to enter the Inns of Court or seek a position with Lord Burghley or the Earl of Leicester, saying that he would consult with his father and adhere to his counsel.

This, together with the writer's need to impress his father-in-law, suggests that he was a relatively young man. If this really was William Marmion it would explain his absence from the Willoughby papers after 1572. No one with the surname Marmion entered any of the Inns of Court between 1557 and 1597.[97] The Willoughby accounts record that in 1584 someone named Marmion gave £40 to the use of Sir Francis Willoughby,[98] the same sum as the annuity given by Bess to the writer of the 24 October letter and its addition, This Marmion may have been William, although at that time Gabriel was still in service with the family. The evidence we have suggests that the man involved in attempts to discredit Sir Francis Willoughby's wife Elizabeth Littleton during the 1570s and his son-in-law Sir Percival Willoughby in the 1580s was Gabriel. He had leased the manor house at Arnold from Sir Francis Willoughby in April 1584 around the time of his marriage to Anne Cooper and appears to have left Wollaton in 1585 and moved to the Arnold property with his new wife who was probably pregnant at the time. Gabriel wrote a letter to Sir Francis Willoughby from London in 1585 regarding Dorothy Willoughby's marriage to Henry Hastings which took place at Wollaton in 1587.[99]

Bess and the Earl of Shrewsbury were not the only couple experiencing marital problems. In 1572, Sir John Littleton, father of Sir Francis Willoughby's wife Elizabeth, wrote to his son-in-law accusing 'Marmyon' of being a principal among those being encouraged by Sir Francis's sister, Margaret, Lady Arundel, to cause the breakdown of his daughter's marriage.[100] Avery Trussell's son John appears to have sided with Lady Willoughby and by referring to the Marmion involved as his 'uncle' makes it clear this was Gabriel.[101] In 1585 Sir Percival Willoughby's father claimed that Sir Francis did little without the counsel of a small clique of servants that included 'Marmyon'.[102] This date, which coincides with Gabriel leaving Wollaton, is the last sixteenth-century entry in the Willoughby papers relating to a Marmion.

Gabriel was once more described as Bess's servant in his marriage settlement of June 1584.[103] Made between Gabriel on the one side and Adam Cooper, citizen and clothworker of London, and Robert Eyre of Blyth Spital (Notts,), the indenture records that Gabriel had agreed to marry Anne Cowper or Cooper, the widow of Robert Cooper, vintner, of St Mary's parish, Nottingham. One of the beneficiaries of Thomas Busby's will was Robert Quarnby of Nottingham, son of Humphrey Quarnby, alderman and three times mayor of the town.[104] The Willoughbys were related to the Thurlands, another of Nottingham's most influential families, who are mentioned several times in the Willoughby papers.[105] It is quite probable that Gabriel knew Robert Cooper. Robert was the son of Thomas Cooper who served as the mayor's sergeant in 1556-7, held the office of bailiff's sergeant in 1574 and sheriff's sergeant the following year.[106]

Robert was town sheriff in 1571-2 and the following year would have been admitted to the Clothing.[107] He became a common councillor of the newly reformed corporation in 1577[108] and undertook military training in 1577 and 1578 with the town's trained bands.[109] A *'Maister* Cowper' living in Nottingham's Long Rowe appears in a list of parishioners of St Mary's parish for April 1582 to April 1583. The use of the prefix 'Maister' indicates this man was a member of the Clothing. This confirms that he was Robert. He is also recorded as not having attended the Clothing since 1582, the year in which he probably died. The list of residents also includes a widow Cowper, then living in The Marshe. This was Robert's widow Anne Cowper. Their son, another Robert, was living in Fishergate.[110] The 'widow Cowper' was Anne Cowper, the woman who went on to marry Gabriel Marmion.[111]

In the marriage indenture, Gabriel agreed to pay certain sums to Anne's seven children from her marriage to Robert. On reaching the age of 21 her two sons, Robert and Adam, were to receive £20 and £60 respectively. On attaining their nineteenth birthdays, the five girls were each to be given £40.[112] In 1584 Anne's children were between the ages of two and sixteen, the eldest having been born in 1568. The couple made their home at a property in Arnold. In 1588, Gabriel may have been the 'Maister Marmeon' of whom Nottingham's Mickletorn Jury made a complaint of his 'settinge the town's ground to a farynar'.[113]

The connections between the Hardwicks, the Marmions, the Willoughbys, and the Greys, were important and helped to shed further light on Bess of Hardwick's life prior to her marriage in 1547 to Sir William Cavendish, a period of which far less is known than of her later years. What is clear is that Henry Marmion, along with other members of his family, played a significant role in the affairs of the Hardwicks.

References and Notes

[1] Paragraph based, except as indicated, on the article on the medieval baronial family contributed by Sir Charles Clay to Complete Peerage, VIII, 505-22.

[2] P. Coss, Robert Marmion (d. 1144), *Oxford Dictionary of National Biography*, 2004, https://doi.org/10.1093/ref:odnb/18081

[3] H. Summerson, *Robert Marmion (d. 1216-18),* Oxford DNB, https://doi.org/10.1093/ref:odnb/18082

[4] C.F.R. Palmer, *History of the Baronial Family of Marmion* (Tamworth) 1875, 117-19; Rev. S. Lodge, Scrivelsby, *The Home of Champions* (London), 1894, 30-42.

[5] Willoughby family, *Oxford Dictionary of National Biography*; University of Nottingham Manuscripts and Special Collections, biog. note on Sir Hugh Willoughby; The Visitation of Nottinghamshire lists Henry as having married an unnamed sister of Robert Willoughby, Visits. Notts. 147. This appears to be an error as it was Henry's father, John, who married Robert Willoughby's sister, Alice.

[6] TNA, C 1/430/18; TNA, C 1/545/3

[7] Northamptonshire Archives, FH 1320.

[8] TNA, STAC 2/25/327-328; STAC 2/33/4; STAC 2/37/4.

[9] A.R. Maddison, *Lincolnshire Pedigrees* (1902), 127-8.

[10] TNA, C 1/852/27-31.

[11] TNA, PROB 11/28/534. Interestingly, Ursula was an Egerton family name and Bridget a Willoughby family name. In his will, Edward did not mention a son of Henry which may indicate that Gabriel was born after 1540.

[12] TNA, PROB 11/15/39.

[13] TNA, REQ 2/6/212.

[14] UNMASC Mi 6/177/96.

[15] TNA, E 150/554/11, E 150/1127/8, C 142/35/31, C 142/37/86.

[16] TNA, C 1/852/21-26, C 1/852/27-31, C 1/861/28, C 1/852/21-26, C 1/861/28.

[17] F. Haselwood, *The Genealogy of the Family of Haselwood: Wickwarren, Belton and Maidwell Branches* (1875), 2-3. John succeeded his father Edmund (d 1548) as Master of the Fleet Prison. See also, n 97.

[18] TNA, C 1/519/55, C 1/427/25; C 1/546/53; C 1/849/9; C 1/861/28, C 1/852/21.

[19] Northamptonshire Archives, FH 1702.

[20] TNA, STAC 2/25/327-328; C 1/849/9; C 1/849/9-13; TNA, C 1/427/25; C 1/852/21; C 1/861/28.

[21] TNA, E 40/14639.

[22] Borthwick Institute for Archives, University of York, 17184384.

[23] UNMASC, biog. note on Sir Hugh Willoughby.

[24] TNA, E 40/10747; E 40/547.

[25] TNA, E 40/547.

[26] UNMASC, biog. note on Sir Henry Willoughby.

[27] P. Riden, 'The Hardwicks of Hardwick Hall in the Fifteenth and Sixteenth Centuries', *Derbyshire Archaeological Journal*, 130 (2010), 146-7.

[28] TNA, E 150/743/8.

[29] HMC Middleton, 307-8.

[30] TNA, STAC 2/17/53.

[31] TNA, STAC 2/17/53; C 146/7541; UNMASC Mi D 403.

[32] HMC Middleton, 338, 353.

[33] TNA, PROB 11/22/542.

[34] HMC Middleton, 314.

[35] Ibid, 315.

[36] Ibid, 317.

[37] UNMASC, Mi 6/175/46.

[38] J.W. Clay (ed.), *North Country Wills*; being abstracts of wills relating to the counties of York, Nottingham, Northumberland, Cumberland, and Westmorland, at Somerset House and Lambeth Palace 1383 (1908), Wills proved in the Prerogative Court of Canterbury, 201; HMC, Middleton, 149. HMC Middleton, 338.

[39] UNMASC, Mi D 1633.

[40] UNMASC, Mi D 810.

[41] UNMASC, biog. note on Sir Henry Willoughby.

[42] J.G. Nichols (ed.), *The Chronicle of Queen Jane and Queen Mary* (Camden Society Old Series, 48, 1850), 66; HMC Middleton, 520, 396-97, 399, 400-3. Lady Grey and her three daughters visited Francis and Margaret Willoughby at Titley on 24/25 October 1550, Mary Grey being described as 'deformed'.

[43] UNMASC, Mi 6/178/49.

[44] UNMASC, biog. note on Sir Francis Willoughby.

[45] e.g. HMC Middleton, 519.

[46] UNMASC Mi C23; UNMASC Mi 6/171/48; HMC Middleton, 161.

[47] D. N. Durant and P. Riden (eds), *The Building of Hardwick Hall, 'Part 2'*, The New Hall, 1591-98 (Derbyshire Record Society 9, 1984), p. xlix.

[48] TNA, C 1/1102/37/9.

[49] We do not know exactly when Jane entered the service of the Carews. The Carews were among West Country evangelical protestants and were related to the Courtneys and closely associated with the Parrs. However, some members of the family remained adherent to the Catholic faith.

[50] TNA, C 142/21/35 in which John Hardwick, Bess's father, is stated as being eleven years old; E 150/743/8; C 142/73/27 (copy in Notts. Archives, DD/P/114/10).

[51] TNA, E 150/743/8.

[52] TNA, STAC 2/7, ff 15-16.

[53] TNA, STAC 2/17/53.

[54] Riden, 'Hardwicks', 152: T. Kilburn, 'The Wardship and Marriage of Robert Barley: First Husband of Bess of Hardwick', DAJ, 134 (2014), 198.

[55] TNA, C 1/1101/17; Kilburn, 'Wardship' 197, 202.

[56] TNA, CP 40/1120.

[57] TNA, C 1/1102/17.

[58] Riden, 'Hardwicks', 152; Kilburn, 'Wardship', 198.

[59] Ibid.

[60] TNA, C 1/1101/17.

[61] TNA, C 1/1365/5-7.

[62] TNA, C 1/102/57-59; C 1/1102/40-41.

[63] TNA, C 1/1102/37/9.

[64] D. N. Durant, *Bess of Hardwick: Portrait of an Elizabethan Dynast* (2008), 12; M. S. Lovell, Bess of Hardwick, First Lady of Chatsworth (2005), 15-26; Riden, 'Hardwicks' 152.

[65] TNA, STAC 4/1/7. I am grateful to Philip Riden for this reference.

[66] TNA, E 150/1161/13; C 142/140/203.

[67] HMC Middleton, 349. In a document dated June 5, 1539, Arthur Barley attempted to make use of the Statute of Uses to avoid feudal dues. He gifted the manors of Barley and Dunstone and all his property in Derbyshire to George Chaworth and Gabriel Barwick. The lands etc. were to be re-conveyed before 24 August to the use of Arthur for life and pass to Robert Barley and his heirs, then to George Barley and his heirs, and then to any of Arthur's heirs. Nottinghamshire Archives, DD/P/CD113. Barwick was Henry Marmion's brother-in-law.

[68] Ibid. 370.

[69] UNMASC, Mi D 167.

[70] HMC Middleton, 416.

[71] Ibid. 317.

[72] Clay, *North Country Wills,* 201.

[73] UNMASC, Mi 2/77/102.

[74] BIA 17184908

[75] HMC Middleton, 149, 560.

[76] TNA, E 150/1161/13; C 142/140/203.

[77] G. W. Marshall (ed.), *The Visitations of the Country of Nottingham in the Years 1569 and 1614* (1871), 181.

[78] Visit. Notts. 76; HMC Middleton, 511 See also TNA, STAC 2/24/182; C 1/412/56; C 2/Eliz/E2/36; C 43/2/34; C 146/11066; C 1/593/13 for further connections between John Egerton and the Willoughbys of Wollaton; UNMASC, biog. note on Sir Henry Willoughby.

[79] Visit. Notts, 28, 147; B. Burke, *The Grand Armoury* (London), 1884, 660.

[80] e.g. UNMASC, Mi 1/3/1-2; Mi 5/169/84, 85, 88 dated 1562; Mi 2/77/102; Mi 6/175/68; HMC Middleton, 127, 515.

[81] BIA 17184908.

[82] TNA, PROB 11/28/534. Gabriel may have been born after Edward's death in 1540 and therefore would not feature in his will.

[83] UNMASC, Mi 6/176/190.

[84] Notts. Archives, 157/DD/P/114/2.

[85] Folger Shakespeare Library, Cavendish-Talbot MSS, X d.428 (102).

[86] UNMASC, Mi C 15; HMC, Middleton, 152-5.

[87] Durant, Bess, 110, 126; Lovell, Bess, 292, 309. The complete breakdown of Bess's marriage to Shrewsbury was evident by late 1583 when she accused her husband of improper conduct in his relations with Mary, Queen of Scots. P. Collinson, *The English Captivity of Mary, Queen of Scots*, Sheffield History Pamphlets, 1987, 34.

[88] HMC Middleton, 542; J. A. M. Cruz, *An Account of an Elizabethan Family: The Willoughbys of Wollaton* (Camden Series, 2019), n. 135. The author's suggestion that William's father may have been Henry Marmion cannot be correct. The writer of the 1582 Chatsworth letter says that he is going to consult his father and that his father was engaged in a dispute with Browne. Henry Marmion died on 4 January 1555. William may have been named for Henry's uncle William.

[89] TNA, C 21/B10/3.

[90] HMC Middleton, 153-5.

[91] TNA, PROB 11/67/450.

[92] TNA, C 21/B10/3.

[93] BIA, Nottingham Act Book. Gabriel Marmion of Arnold, Admin, Jan 1590/1.

[94] UNMASC, 5/169/108-9; Ne D 848.

[95] BIA 17184976.

[96] TNA, C 21/B10/3.

[97] The Records of the Honorable Society of Lincoln's Inn. Admissions and Chapel Registers, The Honourable Society of Lincoln's Inn (London), 1896, vol I, Admissions 1420-1799, 64; J. Foster, Grey's Inn Register of Admissions 1521 - 1889, 61-80; Inner Temple and Grey's Inn admissions online database http://www. innertemplearchives.org.uk/search; H.A.C. Sturgess (ed.), Register of Admissions to the Honourable Society of the Middle Temple, Vol I (1949), 52-63. On 21 Oct 1584, a Marmion Haselwood of Kirklington, Notts, and of Barnards Inn, was admitted to Grays Inn, Foster 66. For relationships between the Marmions and the Haslewoods, see pp

113-115. A contemporary of William Cavendish at Grays Inn was Charles Lennox (Darnley) who became William's brother-in-law and father of Arbella. Henry Willoughby was admitted to Grays Inn in 1573.

[98] Durant, Bess, 117.

[99] UNMASC, Mi 6/170/124/5; Mi 5/169/1/104; Mi 5/169/1/108¬109.

[100] HMC Middleton, 532-33.

[101] Ibid, 550-51.

[102] Ibid, 560-63.

[103] W. H. Stevenson (ed.), Records of the Borough of Nottingham, IV (1889), 417.

[104] UNMASC, Mi 5/169/1/105.

[105] Thomas Thurland married Robert Willoughby's daughter Jane, Visit. Notts. 148; HMC Middleton, 499. See for example HMC Middleton, 120, 455, 457

[106] TNA, STAC 3/10/43 deals with an undated complaint made by Robert More against Ralph Egerton during the reign of Henry VIII. Among the defendants was William Cooper. Ralph was the brother of Henry Marmion's wife, Isabel Egerton; RBN, 50, 419.

[107] The Clothing was the upper house of the town council of Nottingham. Those who served the council in the office of bailiff or sheriff usually entered the ranks of the Clothing after their year of office. The town's seven aldermen were chosen from the ranks of the Clothing. The office of mayor was generally rotated annually from among the aldermen. T. Kilburn, 'Town Government in Elizabethan and Jacobean England: The Corporation of Nottingham, 1558-1625', Birmingham University, B.Soc.Sc dissertation, 1978.

[108] RBN, IV, 409, 419.

[109] Ibid, 179.

[110] Ibid, 419, 422.

[111] Ibid, 209, 202.

[112] UNMASC, Mi 5/169/1/105.

[113] RBN, IV, 222.

7. Hardwick's Royal Princess: Lady Arbella Stuart

Portrait of Arbella Stuart, attrib Marcus Gheerearts by kind permission of the Earl of Strathmore and Kinghorne

Arbella Stuart was the daughter of Charles Stuart, Earl of Lennox, and Elizabeth Cavendish. The exact date of her birth is uncertain. She was probably born in the autumn of 1575 at either Lennox House in Hackney or, possibly, at Chatsworth in Derbyshire. Her father was the younger brother of Henry Darnley, second husband of Mary, Queen of Scots, and father of the future James VI and I. Her mother was the daughter of Elizabeth, Countess of Shrewsbury, better known to history as 'Bess of Hardwick'.

Arbella's parents had been brought together by Margaret Douglas, Dowager Countess of Lennox, and Bess of Hardwick. Neither had sought royal consent for the marriage, and for her pains, Margaret Douglas was to suffer her third spell in the Tower. The daughter of Henry VIII's sister, Margaret Tudor, Margaret Douglas was a granddaughter of Henry VII and first cousin to Elizabeth I. When Bess married her fourth husband George Talbot, Earl of Shrewsbury, in 1567/8 she was already a wealthy woman. In common with women of her rank, she was ambitious for her six surviving children all fathered by her second husband, Sir William Cavendish.

Arbella was niece to Mary, Queen of Scots, and first cousin of James VI of Scotland. She was the only English royal princess in the reign of Elizabeth I. Under English Common Law only someone born in England could inherit English land and/or succeed to the English throne. The law excluding foreigners from the English succession dated back to the reign of Edward III, a law which was laid aside in 1604, the first year of James I's reign. Mary, Queen of Scots, and James VI were born in Scotland.

In a letter of May 1578 to the Archbishop of Glasgow, Mary tried to circumvent the problem by stating that both she and her son, James, had been born 'within the same isle'. Furthermore, shortly before Mary was executed in February 1587 a new law stated that anyone descended from someone who had been found guilty of plotting against the crown could not succeed to the throne. In such circumstances, there were many who came to believe that Arbella Stuart was the legal heir to the English throne.

Although Arbella was raised as a princess of the realm, whatever the ambitions of her grandmothers may have been, she was not to succeed to the crown. However, her story serves to illustrate the importance of succession in early modern England. Following the fall of the Earl of Essex in 1601, Sir Robert Cecil's dominance at court ensured the succession of James VI of Scotland to the English throne in 1603. Arbella's gender was not in her favour, had she been a man she may well have succeeded to the crown. Elizabeth's was a female court.

During the reigns of the Tudor kings, men had been accustomed to holding important and often lucrative court positions, such as that of Gentlemen of the Privy Chamber, which brought with them political power and status through which they could influence royal policy. This was not so in Elizabeth's court in which many such roles were given to women. Indeed, Elizabeth strictly forbade her court ladies to engage in matters of state. By the time Elizabeth's long reign drew to a close, many powerful men had tired of a female court and wanted a return to the male-dominated court life of Henry VIII and Edward VI.

Despite his many years of service to Queen Elizabeth, William Cecil always believed that a king was preferable to a queen, a view shared by his son, Sir Robert Cecil. Bess of Hardwick was careful to maintain good relations with the Cecils. Although William Cecil had once championed the claims of the Greys and their offspring, by the 1590s both he and his son, Robert, chose to back the Stuart claim not in the shape of Arbella but in that of James VI of Scotland. Unlike Mary, Queen of Scots, Arbella did not have the support of English Catholics or powerful countries such as France or Spain.

Marriage became a major issue in Arbella's life. Any prospective husband would have had to have been of suitably high rank. Bess of Hardwick's fourth husband, George Talbot, Earl of Shrewsbury, claimed that Bess had tried hard to persuade him to seek a marriage for Arbella with almost every high-ranking family in England. In 1581, Elizabeth I considered marrying Arbella to Esme Stuart (d 1583) but in 1583, at the age of eight, Arbella was betrothed to the three-year-old Lord Denbigh, son of royal favourite Robert Dudley, Earl of Leicester.

In a letter to the French ambassador, Mary, Queen of Scots, claimed that the proposal to marry Arbella to Robert was conceived by Bess. The Spanish ambassador, noting that Arbella was Queen Elizabeth's 'nearest heiress', saw this as an attempt by Leicester, and his wife, Lettice, to gain the throne for his son. However, 'Little Robert, the Noble Imp', as he was known, died in 1584.

Queen Elizabeth toyed with the idea of James VI as a potential husband for Arbella. As tensions with Philip II of Spain grew in the 1580s, in 1587, Elizabeth looked to marry Arbella to Rainutio Farnese, the son of the Duke of Parma, a proposal she revived in 1591. Possibly as a means of settling the dispute over the Lennox earldom, in 1588 and 1589 James VI proposed a marriage between Arbella and Esme Stuart's son, Ludovic Stuart, Duke of Lennox, but this came to nothing.

In 1590, rumour had it that Arbella was to marry Henry Percy, Earl of Northumberland, and in 1596 Pope Clement VIII proposed Rainutio Farnese's brother as a husband for Arbella. In 1599, Robert Cecil suggested a match with Duke Mathias of Austria. The Prince of Conde, nephew to Henri IV of France, was considered in 1601 and in 1609 there were rumours of a marriage between Arbella and the Duke of Moldova.

Nothing ever came of these and other marriage proposals. Neither Elizabeth I nor James I wanted Arbella to marry as her closeness to the English throne meant that children from a marriage could potentially become—as indeed Arbella was herself—rivals for the English throne. For much of her reign, Elizabeth I used the prospect of her hand in marriage as a political bargaining tool. As the queen aged beyond child-bearing years and her intention never to marry became obvious to all, this strategy became less viable. From the 1590s Arbella became a pawn in the Queen's foreign policy as a marriage with her was substituted for one with Elizabeth. After Elizabeth's death in 1603, James I had no more desire to see Arbella married than had Elizabeth before him and he ensured Arbella's dependence by depriving her of money and patrimony.

Arbella's father died the year after her birth. Up to the age of three and a half, she was raised by her mother and paternal grandmother, Margaret Douglas. She first attended court at the age of three. After Margaret's death in 1578, Arbella, probably with her mother, moved to Chatsworth. She was well educated speaking six languages including Latin, Italian and French, and like Queen Elizabeth, she wrote in an elegant italic hand. She studied the Bible and the classics, played the virginals and the lute, learned dancing and embroidery and, like other members of her family, became a skilled horsewoman.

During her early years, time was spent with her cousins, the children of her aunt Mary, wife of Gilbert Talbot. Arbella's mother died in 1582 and Bess became her granddaughter's guardian. In 1587, at the age of twelve, Arbella returned to court. Possibly to annoy the Spanish, Elizabeth is said to have let it be known to the French ambassador that the day would come when Arbella would occupy the same position as Elizabeth herself. In 1588, Arbella became a Lady-in-Waiting to the Queen but was suddenly ordered back to Derbyshire to be kept under the watchful eye of her grandmother, Bess of Hardwick.

In 1603, the Venetian ambassador was to claim that Arbella was dismissed from court by Elizabeth for seeking precedence over the other court ladies. There may have been some truth to this, but the reminiscence came fifteen years after the event at a time when there were those at James I's court, including the ambassador himself, seeking to discredit Arbella. Another explanation for Arbella's abrupt removal from court is that this was the period of the Spanish Armada and there were fears she might be kidnapped and used as a figurehead by those seeking to replace Elizabeth as queen. Aged sixteen, Arbella returned to court with Bess in 1591 during the revived Farnese marriage proposals. It has been suggested that in 1592 Arbella was abruptly ordered to leave court by Elizabeth because she was rumoured to be getting too close to the Queen's favourite, Robert Devereaux, Earl of Essex.

It is likely that the earl was simply using Arbella as a pawn in his own political intrigues. The Queen ordered her to return to Derbyshire. This should not be interpreted simply as Elizabeth acting out of jealousy. The attention Essex was showing towards one so close to the throne was a real danger. This threat to Elizabeth's security was not lost on the Cecils or Elizabeth herself.

The discovery of a suspected plot to kidnap Arbella provided the pretext for Arbella's removal from court, and from Essex. For the remaining eleven years of Elizabeth's reign, Arbella was kept far from court under the close supervision of her grandmother. When Elizabeth died on March 24, 1603, Arbella was expected to lead the funeral procession but refused saying that the old Queen had not wanted her in life so she would not have her in death.

The years 1587 to 1591 may have brought about a significant shift in Bess's ambitions for Arbella. The 1587 execution of Mary, Queen of Scots, demonstrated the dangers facing anyone who sought to usurp Elizabeth's crown. The following year saw the death of Bess's great friend and ally Robert Dudley, Earl of Leicester, and the emergence of plots in which Arbella replaced Mary Stuart as a focal point. Add to this Essex's so-called dalliance with Arbella and it is no surprise that Elizabeth ordered Arbella's removal from court. Like Mary Stuart before her, Arbella would be less of a threat in far-off Derbyshire. It is probable that Bess, too, came to recognise the dangers now facing her granddaughter and may have abandoned any ambition to see Arbella as Elizabeth's successor. Bess became determined to protect her granddaughter from those, who would come to include her eldest son, Henry, willing to use Arbella as a focus for their plots.

Banishment from court and isolation in Derbyshire was to have a profound effect on Arbella. For much of her early adult life, Arbella was largely confined in Derbyshire with little or no company of her own age and rank. It is said that at Hardwick New Hall she was eventually forced to sleep in the same bedchamber as her grandmother. In keeping a close eye on Arbella, Bess was not merely following the instructions of the Queen and the Privy Council but as the task grew more onerous, she more than once asked to be relieved of the responsibility. The move from the old hall into Hardwick New Hall took place in 1597 by which time Bess was in her mid-seventies.

Her view of the world had been shaped in the middle decades of the sixteenth century and as that century ended her attitudes would have doubtless seemed outdated, out-of-touch, to a young woman in her twenties who longed for marriage as an escape from her enforced isolation. In late 1602, with no prospect of marriage in sight, Arbella came up with a scheme to marry Edward Seymour, the sixteen-year-old grandson of the ageing Earl of Hertford and his wife Katherine Grey (d. 1568). The Grey sisters—Jane, Katherine, and Mary—were granddaughters of Henry VIII's sister, Mary. Arbella was the great-granddaughter of Henry VIII's sister, Margaret, and both she and the Grey sisters, were descended from Henry VII. Why Arbella set her sights on Edward is unclear. It has been suggested that a match with the Seymours may have been considered at some earlier date.

Arbella seems to have developed an affinity with Lady Jane Grey, both women being ill-used by men seeking to put them on the throne in place of another. Hertford was the son of Protector Somerset and the nephew of Queen Jane Seymour, mother of Edward VI. He had married Catherine Grey in 1560 but the marriage had taken place without the Queen's permission. Elizabeth had the marriage declared void and their two sons deemed illegitimate. Despite the taint of illegitimacy, under the terms of Henry VIII's will, Edward had some pretentions to the throne. Any offspring from a marriage to Arbella would have certainly had a very strong claim to the crown but having suffered greatly at Elizabeth's hands for his own marriage and fearful that a similar fate might befall his grandson the old earl immediately reported Arbella's scheme to the authorities.

Sir Henry Brounker, the queen's commissioner, was sent to Hardwick by Sir Robert Cecil to investigate matters. Brounker was an associate of the Thynnes and Bayntons, members of the West Country affinity which included the St Loes. Bess had almost certainly known the Brounkers for many years. Her son, William Cavendish, married his second wife, Elizabeth Wortley, in 1604. Elizabeth was the mother of Francis Wortley, her eldest child by her first husband. In November 1610, Francis married Henry Brounker's niece, Grace Brounker, the fourth daughter of Henry's elder brother Sir William Brounker.

In February 1603, Arbella again attempted an escape from Bess by declaring her real lover was not Edward Seymour but her cousin, James VI of Scotland.

Brounker was again despatched to Hardwick. Both episodes can be seen as desperate attempts by Arbella to secure a release from confinement. In her efforts to persuade Brounker to recommend her removal from Hardwick, she penned lengthy, rambling depositions that became so badly scrawled as to be virtually illegible. At one stage, she began a hunger strike. Brounker's reports speak of Arbella's mood swings, tantrums, bursting into tears and saying all would be well if she could be released from her grandmother's care.

Having failed to convince Brounker to order her removal from Hardwick, Arbella became involved in an even more daring plan of escape. Most likely with the foreknowledge of his sister Mary and, possibly, her husband, Gilbert Talbot, on March 10, 1603, Arbella's uncle, Henry Cavendish, and a company of armed retainers, including a prominent catholic, rode up to the gates of Hardwick with the intention of 'rescuing' Arbella. The fracas drew a crowd of astonished onlookers. Bess ordered the gates to be kept locked, whilst from outside the walls, Arbella could be heard screaming that she was a prisoner. The whole affair ended with Henry riding away from Hardwick empty-handed.

To what extent this attempt to secure Arbella's release was related to rumours of Elizabeth I's closeness to death is unknown, but it seems likely. Sir Robert Cecil almost certainly saw it as part of a plan hatched by those against the Scottish succession and the remnants of the old Essex faction to place Arbella among 'friends' and it led to an investigation which saw Henry Cavendish summoned before the Privy Council. Being so desperate to get away from Hardwick, it is possible that Arbella may not have been aware of the very grave position into which she had placed herself, but Bess would have certainly recognised the dangers and it was at this time, in a letter to Sir Henry Brounker, dated that same 10 March 1603 that in an effort to protect both Arbella and perhaps herself, Bess was to describe Henry Cavendish as 'my bad sonne Henry'. Nevertheless, ten days later Bess removed both Henry and Arbella from her will.

Significantly, just days before Elizabeth I's death, William Cavendish had Arbella moved to Oldcoates, a smaller property easier to defend than Hardwick's halls. He ordered muskets, powder and shot from London at the considerable cost of £80. Weapons and armour were also acquired from neighbours. Arbella was confined to the house under armed guard. William's most trusted servants were ordered to keep a lookout for any strangers arriving in the area. William clearly feared that another attempt would be made to secure Arbella's person by those opposed to James VI's succession.

News of the old queen's death reached Hardwick within days and William rode into Chesterfield to hear James proclaimed king. A few weeks later William and his son attended on the new king at York. Arbella's fortunes seemed to improve with the death of Elizabeth I. King James was aware of and had some sympathy for his cousin's plight. He ordered that she be allowed to leave Hardwick and be placed under the care of Henry. Grey, Earl of Kent, at Wrest Park in Bedfordshire.

By May 1603, Arbella, now aged 28 and still unmarried, was at court and then housed at Sheen. It was at this time that two plots were discovered, the Main Plot and the Bye Plot. Not everyone was happy with the succession of the Scottish king to the English throne. In particular, the remnants of the defeated Essex faction resented the power that Cecil was now exercising under the new regime.

The Bye Plot and the more serious Main Plot are little known, mainly because they have become overshadowed by the more famous Gunpowder Treason of 1605. The Main Plot involved Lord Cobham and, allegedly, Sir Walter Raleigh. Its intended result was the assassination of King James and Sir Robert Cecil. Arbella was to be married to Lord Grey of Wilton and be placed on the throne. Henry Cavendish was implicated in the Bye Plot and ordered to appear before the Privy Council.

It is possible that Arbella, however unwittingly, had come perilously close to involvement in something of a similar nature just two months earlier even though her only motive at that time had been to escape from Hardwick. She must have become aware, much as Bess herself had been aware, of the dangers of allowing herself to be manipulated by others as a rival for the crown for as soon as she had knowledge of the scheme, she herself reported the plot to Cecil. It is one of the great ironies that Arbella came to constitute such a threat to James in the same way that his mother had posed a threat to Elizabeth I.

Despite being on good terms with Queen Anne and her son, Prince Henry, Arbella was not particularly enamoured by the shallow nature of James I's court. Yet her future, and this included her marriage, was in the hands of her royal cousin. Arbella may have been freed from what she saw as isolation and confinement at Hardwick, but she was still not free to marry.

When Bess first made her Last Will and Testament dated 25 April 1601, she bequeathed to Arbella 'all my pearls and jewels which I shall have at the time of my decease except such as shall be otherwise bequeathed'. On 10 March 1603,

Henry Cavendish had attempted to release Arbella from Hardwick. On March 20, Bess added a codicil to her will which disinherited both Henry and Arbella. However, in March 1605 Arbella was able to make a rare return to Hardwick. She had obtained an open letter from James I for the creation of a peer of her choice. She knew full well that Bess would not be able to resist the temptation of acquiring the title of Baron Cavendish for her favourite son, Arbella's uncle, William, even if it did come with a £2000 price tag.

Bess had not wanted her granddaughter to come to Hardwick and Arbella was concerned about the kind of reception she would receive. She persuaded King James to write to Bess to smooth the way for the visit to take place. Bess questioned why someone who had so recently been desperate to escape from Hardwick was now so desirous to return. Nonetheless, a degree of reconciliation did take place and Arbella left with gifts of a gold cup and £300. However, on 15 August 1607 Bess added a second codicil to her will which confirmed the codicil of 1603. Arbella arrived at Hardwick two days after her grandmother's funeral.

There exists an incomplete list dated 23 February 1608 of the jewels given to her by William Cavendish before she returned to London. William must have ignored the codicils added to Bess's will and may, as Bess had originally intended, have given his niece those pearls and jewels not otherwise bequeathed elsewhere in his mother's will. It has been suggested that the strings of pearls worn by Arbella in a portrait currently dated to c1605 may be Bess's pearls seen in the portrait on page 142. However, for that to be the case, the portrait of Arbella would almost certainly have had to have been painted after February 1608. By early 1609, Arbella, now in her middle thirties, was suspected of seeking a marriage with the Duke of Moldova but this was more likely a ruse to hide her renewed involvement with the Seymours, this time with Edward Seymour's twenty-two-year-old younger brother, William. Arbella was arrested and questioned about the Moldova marriage but in the end appears to have been under the impression that, although James I would not favour a foreign match for her, he would look more favourably on a marriage to a loyal Englishman. She received an increase in her personal allowance and seemed to have returned to royal favour when, despite warnings from the Privy Council, she and William Seymour married secretly at 4:00 a.m. on 22 June 1610, a legal marriage but one which did not have royal consent.

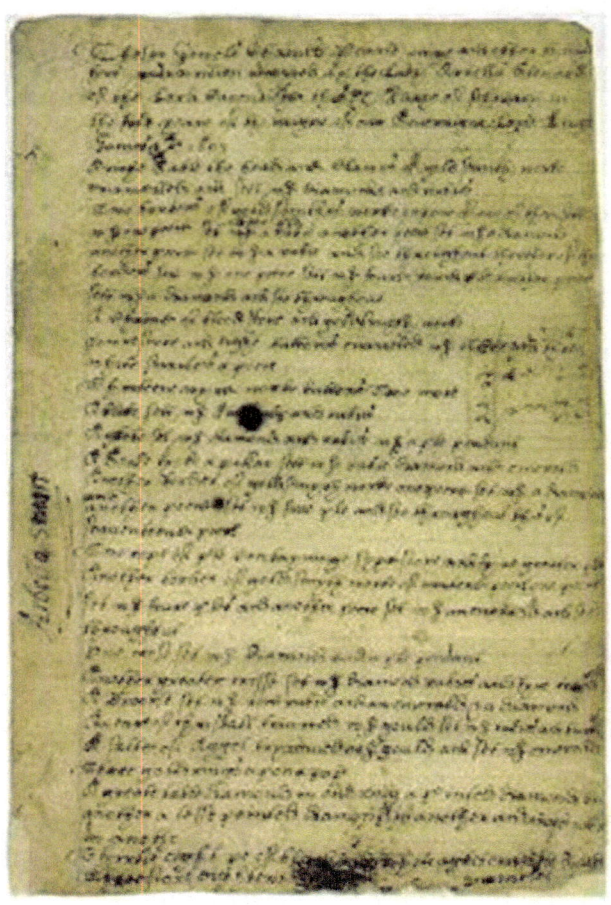

List of jewels given to Arbella, signed by her, 23 February 1608. D.1897/1
©Derbyshire Record Office

Some historians believe that at the time of these events James I may have suffered an attack of porphyria and that this helps explain his harsh treatment of the newlyweds. By 8 July, William was in the Tower and the next day Arbella was placed under house arrest in Sir Thomas Parry's house at Lambeth. James was determined to keep them apart probably to prevent any possibility of children whose claims to the English crown would potentially be greater than his own. A child from the marriage of Arbella and William would bring together the lines of Henry VIII's two sisters, Margaret and Mary Tudor. James decided to remove Arbella to distant Durham where she was to be placed in the custody of the bishop.

In March 1611, Arbella set out on the long journey north, but she did not get very far. The first night's stop was to be at Barnet, but delays meant it was in fact spent at Highgate where Arbella apparently became ill. James sent one of his own doctors, Dr Hammond, to attend her. Hammond recommended she be moved to East Barnet where she was placed in the hands of Sir James Croft. Arbella's sickness, feigned or genuine, delayed the departure for Durham for almost twelve weeks.

The king set a final deadline of Wednesday, June 5. James seems to have interpreted Arbella's actions as sheer obstinacy and was determined that he would be obeyed. He may have been intending to teach his headstrong cousin a lesson for on more than one occasion Arbella was led to understand that after a short stay in the north, the king's intention was to restore her to favour. She seems to have given little credence to such reports and, in any case, Durham was much too far away from her husband.

In an act worthy of a Shakespearian heroine, between two and three in the afternoon of Monday, June 3, Arbella left the house at East Barnet disguised in men's clothing, including rapier, and walked half a mile to an inn where horses were saddled and ready. By 6:00 pm, she had ridden the 14 miles to another inn at Blackwall where William was supposedly waiting, his luggage was there but there was no sign of the man himself. Boats were boarded to take Arbella and her party downriver to a French ship which was to convey her and her husband to France but there was still no sign of William. Arbella spent the night in a boat and next morning boarded the French ship. She still wanted to wait for William, but the captain insisted they set sail otherwise the tide would be missed.

William made his escape from the Tower disguised in a black wig and beard. He simply walked out of the West Gate following a cart but had set out later than planned and missed meeting up with the French ship and his wife. There was no contingency plan. William was able to find another ship and set sail but by this time their escape was known, and James had sent ships after them. Arbella's ship lingered off Calais waiting for any sign of William but the ships that arrived were those sent by James with orders to detain the newlyweds and return them to England.

Arbella was taken back to London and placed in the Tower. His first attempt thwarted by storms, William had by this time landed at Ostend and was to remain abroad until after Arbella's death. Once back in England, he married Frances

Devereaux, a daughter of the Earl of Essex, and within months was restored to royal favour. He was to name his eldest daughter, Arbella.

Languishing in the Tower, Arbella was yet again illegally deprived of her freedom. She was soon joined by her aunt Mary, Countess of Shrewsbury, who had masterminded the escape from East Barnet. In all, twelve people were arrested for their alleged part in the conspiracy. Arbella was never charged. It was enough for James that she had disobeyed him and all attempts to persuade him to release his cousin were ignored. Arbella's aunt, Mary, a known catholic, tried to persuade her to convert to the old faith. Instead, Arbella managed to obtain a copy of the key to her room and, rather than use it to escape, sent it to James I as a demonstration of her loyalty.

The death of James I's eldest son, Prince Henry on 6 November 1612 brought Arbella another step closer to the throne. The new heir, Prince Charles, was known to have health problems. In 1613, there appear to have been at least two plots to free Arbella from the Tower, one of which cost her the loss of several valuable pearls. Both plots, however, came to nothing. Arbella herself also seems to have conceived a scheme to fake the death and burial of William Seymour so that he could be brought to the Tower where husband and wife could secretly live together. In 1613, she entertained false hopes that she would be released to attend the marriage of James I's daughter, Elizabeth.

As months of confinement turned into years of confinement, Arbella came to feel there would be no release. She took to her bed on 8 September 1614: she would either be released from the Tower, or she would die there. Over the next twelve months, as Catherine Grey had done before her, Arbella refused medical attention and sustenance. Her health deteriorated and she died in the Tower on 25 September 1615 at the age of just forty. There was to be no royal funeral but, on the king's order, her body was placed in the same Westminster Abbey vault as that of Mary, Queen of Scots, close to the coffin of James's son, Prince Henry.

There are those, both during Arbella's lifetime and since, who have argued that her actions betray a strain of madness. There is little doubt that as a young woman Arbella's desperate desire to marry, and through marriage escape what she saw as unjust confinement in the hands of a woman who herself had had four husbands, produced periods of immense psychological stress that could easily have been interpreted as madness. Reading Brounker's reports Robert Cecil came to question Arbella's sanity, but it suited his purpose to do so. He was already working to secure the succession of James VI to the English throne. Even though Cecil had probably concluded that she was not seeking the crown for herself, Arbella remained a potential threat to the success of his plans. In 1603, the Venetians reported that Arbella was, or was at least pretending to be, half-mad but had their own reasons for doing so.

Arbella's bouts of so-called madness seem to have coincided with periods of extreme anxiety. Perhaps she suffered what in more recent times are referred to as stress-related illnesses or 'nervous breakdowns.' Some historians have gone further by suggesting that Arbella was a victim of porphyria, a condition more famously associated with the alleged 'madness' of King George III, who was himself a descendant of James I. The disease has many symptoms including speedy recovery from bouts of mental instability, hysteria, vomiting, discoloured urine, sore eyes, and severe headaches to the front of the head. Other symptoms include diarrhoea, uncontrolled weeping, sensitivity to light, pain in the sides and weakness of the muscles.

We should avoid the pitfall of assuming that anyone displaying such symptoms was necessarily a victim of the disease, but Arbella's known symptoms do point to a possible diagnosis of variegate porphyria. Porphyria tends to be more prevalent in women of child-bearing age and is believed to have been present in the Stuart line. James I and his mother, Mary, Queen of Scots, are thought by some to have suffered from the disease. If porphyria was indeed the curse of the Stuarts how then did it get into Arbella's bloodline? The most likely answer would seem to be via her paternal grandfather, Matthew Stuart, a descendant of James II of Scotland.

However, recently medical historians have begun to suggest that rather than being a victim of porphyria George III suffered from bipolar disorder, a disease which can manifest itself in very similar symptoms to those of porphyria. Arbella certainly displayed such symptoms. It is possible that rather than being a victim of porphyria, Arbella may have suffered from bipolar disorder.

Was Arbella truly insane or simply misunderstood? Was she a victim of porphyria or was she bipolar? Perhaps we will never be sure for certain. It is well known that at the time of her death, Elizabeth I could not speak. Her deathbed was encircled by Cecil and members of the Cecil faction and, as the story goes, a list of possible successors was read out to the dying monarch who raised her hand at the mention of James's name. We only have the word of those who were present when the old Queen supposedly signalled that James should succeed her to the throne.

These men had a vested interest in securing the English throne for the Scottish king. What we do know is that the Duc de Sully, chief minister of Henri IV of France, who visited England in 1601, was to recall that it was common knowledge at that time that the English crown belonged rightfully to Arbella, a crown she was destined never to wear.

Further Reading

Armitage. J. (2017) *Arbella Stuart: The Uncrowned Queen,* Amberley.

Bradley. E. T. (2007) *Life of the Lady Arabella Stuart: Containing a Biographical Memoir and a Collection of Her Letters,* 2 vols, Kessinger Publishing.

Durant. David. N. (1978) *Bess of Hardwick: Portrait of an Elizabethan Dynast,* Weidenfield and Nicolson, London.

Durant. David. N. (1978) *Arbella Stuart: A Rival to the Queen,* Weidenfield and Nicolson, London.

Gristwood. S. (2003) *Arbella: England's Lost Queen,* Bantam Books, London.

Hardy. Blanche, C. (1913) *Arbella Stuart: A Biography*, Kessinger Publishing.

Lovell. M. S. (2005) *Bess of Hardwick: The First Lady of Chatsworth.*

Norrington. R. (2002) *In the Shadow of the Throne* (Peter Owen), London.

Steen. S. J. (ed) (1994) *The Letters of Lady Arbella Stuart,* O.U.P, Oxford.

My Bess: A Woman of Her Time

©National Trust Images/John Hammond

Bess of Hardwick has been shackled to a historiography that began with Volume 3 of Sir William Dugdale's *An Historical Account of the Lives and most Memorable Actions of Our English Nobility* published in the mid-1670s. Dugdale established the foundation for future biographers. However, by stripping away some of the long-held and oft-repeated myths old and new, a different interpretation emerges from that presented by previous authors.

Dugdale was writing around one and a half centuries after Bess's birth and some seven decades or so after her death by which time few, if any, of Bess's contemporaries were alive. Then, as now, very little was known about Bess's early life. Dugdale needed to explain how a woman from such a relatively undistinguished background as Bess ended her life as a countess, a woman who, after acquiring her Talbot dower from Gilbert in 1591, was reputedly second only in wealth to Queen Elizabeth.

According to Dugdale, Bess's four marriages brought her great wealth. He writes that Robert Barley's:

...great affections to her [i.e., Bess], she made such advantage; that, for lack of issue by her, he settled a large inheritance in lands upon her self and her heirs; which, by his death, within a short time after, she fully enjoyed...

However, we know this was not the case. Dugdale goes on to tell us that Bess's marriage to Sir William Cavendish produced six surviving children. He skips over the fact that at the time of his death, Sir William owed a huge sum to the crown and that Bess was left facing a parliamentary bill for the recovery of that debt and alleged imminent destitution.

Turning to the St Loe marriage Dugdale claims that Bess:

...surviving Sir William Cavendish; and, discerning her self still youthful and amiable, and likewise courted by many; she made choice of Sir William St Lo, Knight (though much superior to her in years) then Captain of the Guard to Queen Elizabeth, and possessor of divers faire Lordships in Glocestershire. With whom she made such termes, in order to her Marriage with him, as that she fixt the Inheritance thereof, upon her self and her own heirs (for fault of issue by him) excluding his own daughters and brothers.

Dugdale here asserts that Bess's marriage to St Loe took place only on the condition set by Bess that he would leave his entire fortune to her. Dugdale was obviously aware that Sir William left his fortune to Bess but did not know the precise details and circumstances of that arrangement. In a will dated 1544, Sir John St Loe had bequeathed annuities to his four sons and their sister. In his final will of 1551, Sir John made no further provision for Sir William's three younger brothers and sister. Having failed to reach any agreement over their father's estate with his much-distrusted brother Edward, Sir William's will merely sought to reaffirm the position created by his father's will of 1551.

Stating that Bess insisted on inheriting St Loe's fortune before she would agree to marry him served simply to support Dugdale's assertion that Bess "...became Mistriss of a very vast fortune, by her successful matching with several wealthy Husbands." Dugdale's statement that St Loe had two daughters may also mislead. Based on information provided by Edward St Loe's descendants, the 1623 visitation records inform us that William St Loe died without issue. It was commonplace for a husband or wife to refer to the children of an earlier marriage, and to illegitimate children, as being their own sons or daughters. In her letters to Gilbert Talbot, Bess frequently refers to him as 'my son Gilbert'. The two daughters to whom Dugdale refers were most likely Elizabeth and Mary Cavendish, the two daughters of Bess and Sir William Cavendish who remained unmarried at the time of Bess's marriage to St Loe.

When it comes to Bess's marriage to George Talbot, Dugdale tells us that she pulled off the same trick because Talbot...

...was captivated with her beauty; she stood upon such termes with him; that, unless he would yield; that Gilbert, then his second son, but afterwards his heir, should take Mary her daughter to wife; and that Henry her eldest son, should marry the Lady Grace his youngest daughter; besides the setling of a large Joynture in Lands upon her self, he must not enjoy her. Unto all which he condiscending (and much more after) became her.

It is difficult to accept the notion that a man like George Talbot, who did not need an heir, would have been allured by the 'beauty' of a 46-year-old thrice widowed woman who had borne the rigours of childbirth eight times in a single decade. At the time of her marriage to Talbot, Gilbert's elder brother, Lord Francis Talbot, was still alive. Without the benefit of hindsight Bess could not possibly have known that Gilbert would ultimately succeed to his father's titles and estates. In terms of jointures, Bess had jointure on the Cavendish inheritance but in 1584 this didn't stop Talbot from forcing her to leave Chatsworth leaving Henry Cavendish, who was to inherit the Cavendish estates on Bess's death, in the invidious position of having to support Talbot or his mother. Bess may have been the one to insist on prenuptial agreements that the St Loe inheritance was to pass to Charles Cavendish and later that the Hardwick inheritance passed to William Cavendish. In doing so, she was merely protecting the inheritances of her sons rather than consciously laying the foundations of a dynasty.

Reading Dugdale's view of Bess it becomes clear that within a few decades of her death, the idea of her being a rapacious dynast was alive and well, laying the path for future commentators and biographers. In his manuscript *History of the Talbot Family* of 1692, the antiquary Nathaniel Johnson claimed he had been informed by two aged men that Bess met and married Robert Barley in London when both were in service to Lady Zouche of Codnor. Apparently, Johnson's informants told him that Bess attended and cared for a sickly Robert and the latter fell in love with and married her. Johnson claimed that Bess prevailed upon Robert Barley to settle his estate on her and her heirs such that after he died, she inherited a large estate. Those two aged men must have been exceptionally old to recall events that happened a century and a half previously.

At best, they could only have been providing Johnson with hearsay and the fact is we only have Johnson's word that he was told anything by anybody. We have already shown that Bess did not inherit a substantial estate from her first husband. It is possible that, like her sister Jane, Bess could have entered into service, possibly at Codnor, before she was espoused but the fact is that there is no definitive evidence to show that Bess—or Robert Barley—was ever in service to the Zouches. To complicate things further, there were two Lady Zouches at Codnor at the time Bess was supposed to be in the family's service. Johnson's informants failed to identify exactly which Lady Zouche, Lady Anne or the aged Lady Margaret (nee Willoughby), they, and thus he, had in mind.

Sir George Zouche and Anne Gainsford had only taken possession of Codnor Castle early in the 1540s and may have been requiring additional household servants. The Zouches would have been considered an appropriate family of suitable rank in which Bess could be placed but this was also true of the Willoughbys and the Greys. The most likely would appear to have been the Greys.

From Johnson, let us turn our attention to Arthur Collins whose *Historical Collections of the Noble Families of Cavendishe, Holles, Vere, Harley, and Ogle* was published in 1752. Following Dugdale's lead, Collins describes Bess as 'beautiful and discreet' and tells us that she married Robert Barley when she was fourteen years of age. When Robert died on the '2nd of February 1542 24 HVIII' Bess inherited his large estate. The 24th year of Henry VIII's regnal calendar ran from 22 April 1532 to 21 April 1533. Using New Style dating this means Collins dates Robert's death to February 1533.

However, we know that Robert was born in January 1530 and died at the end of 1544. Furthermore, for Collins to be right Bess would have to have been born in 1519. In fact, the Barley inheritance passed to Robert's younger brother George and Bess was forced to struggle for several years through both Common Law and Equity Courts after Robert's death in order to secure her Barley dower.

Collins goes on to tell us that Sir William Cavendish had a 'great affection' for Bess and that she simply had to use her charms to persuade him to relocate to Derbyshire and commence the building of Chatsworth. Like Dugdale, Collins tells us that Bess used her beauty, charm and wit, to captivate and beguile her husbands before conning them into handing over their inheritances. Conveniently failing to note that, by the time of Talbot's marriage to Bess, jointures had commonly replaced dowries, Collins tells us that Talbot was so smitten by Bess that she easily persuaded him to yield jointure to her and agreed to the marriage of his son Gilbert to her daughter Mary Cavendish. Collins wondered whether there had ever been a case for:

...one woman to be four times a happy and creditable Wife; to rise by every Husband unto greater Wealth, and higher Honours; to have an Unanimous Issue by one Husband only; to have all those children live, and all, by her Advice, be honourably, and creditably, disposed of in her lifetime and, after all, to live Seventeen Years a widow, in absolute Power and Plenty.

Dugdale and Collins present Bess as a consummate, calculating, confidence trickster. Putting aside the question of how feminine beauty was defined in the sixteenth century, we might ask why her husbands—or in this context victims—would have been so naive as to have fallen for such blatant trickery. It is hard to imagine men such as Sir William Cavendish, Sir William St Loe, and George Talbot, would have been so foolish. We have no images of a young Bess and one suspects neither did Dugdale. He had to come up with some explanation of how Bess had acquired her wealth and he did.

Collins and later commentators simply followed suit. Oddly, Collins states that Bess became a widow for the fourth time on 18 November 1609 that is over a year and a half after her own death. He fails to note that two of Sir William's daughters by Bess did not reach adulthood. Collins also fails to recognise that multiple weddings were a common feature among Elizabethan nobles, including the Talbots.

Edmund Lodge published the second edition of his *Illustrations of British History* in 1838. In Volume II, we are once again informed that Bess prevailed upon Robert Barley to settle his estate on her and her heirs. Lodge notes there was no issue from Robert's marriage to Bess such that the heirs who would ultimately benefit from this arrangement would be the offspring of a potential future marriage, in this instance Bess's marriage to Sir William Cavendish. Lodge repeats the story that Bess persuaded St Loe to sign over his inheritance to her but adds that this was 'to the utter prejudice of his two daughters by a former wife'. Bess then completed her 'conquests' by drawing Shrewsbury…

…into the same disgraceful and imprudent concessions which she had procured from his unlucky predecessors; and, partly by entreaties, partly by threats, induced him to sacrifice, in a great measure, the fortune, interest, and happiness, of himself and his family to the aggrandisement of her children by Sir William Cavendish.

However, we have evidence to show that William St Loe died without issue. The two daughters mentioned by Lodge were probably the children of Sir William Cavendish. I offer no apology for quoting in full Lodge's summation of Bess's character. She was, he says,

a woman of masculine understanding and conduct, proud, furious, selfish and unfeeling. She was a builder, buyer and seller of estates, a money-lender, a farmer, and a merchant of lead, coal and timber; when disengaged from these employments, she intrigued alternatively with Elizabeth and Mary, always to the terror and prejudice of her husband. She lived to a great old age, continually flattered, but seldom deceived, and died in 1607 [Old Style dating, 1608 New Style], immensely rich, and without a friend.

Edmund Lodge re-hashed a good deal of what Dugdale, Johnson, and Collins had written. He added little to what was already known of Bess's marriages and repeated a good deal that was inaccurate. In his 1819 *Hallamshire*, Joseph Hunter carried on where Edmund Lodge had left off, once more presenting Bess as a charmer and chancer who callously ruined her fourth husband. In her 1881 catalogue of portraits at Longleat, Mary Louise Boyle informs her readers that Bess was a 'beautiful, vivacious, practical and headstrong' woman who at the age of 14, 'married Mr Barlow, a rich country gentleman'. Well, not quite as this would have meant Bess had to have been born in 1529. Not so.

In his *The Sisters of Lady Jane Grey and their Wicked Grandfather*, published in 1912, the antiquarian Richard Davey informed his readers that seeing no hope of a suitable marriage Bess wrote to Lady Zouch and shortly thereafter, without a word to her family, she ran away to London to join the said lady's household. It was there that she met the 70-year-old 'John' Barley (*pace* Robert) whom she nursed and married. He died soon after and left Bess his entire, considerable fortune. So, the nonsense continued.

We can demonstrate that all these accounts contain many fundamental errors. Therefore, we cannot take anything they say for granted or assume the accounts are accurate. Such authors set in train many of the myths that continue to appear in modern biographies and commentaries. Despite a degree of revision and rehabilitation, in one way or another modern biographers persist with the view that Bess was a rapacious and unyielding dynast.

So, what about my Bess? The weight of the evidence suggests that Bess was born into a minor Derbyshire gentry family around 1521/22. Her father's will refers to his daughters but they are not named individually. In the mid-1530s, both Ralph Leche, Bess's stepfather and close family associate, Henry Marmion, claimed that they had purchased Robert Barley's marriage and wardship from Robert's father, Arthur Barley, probably with the intent of marrying Robert to one of John Hardwick's daughters, most likely Bess. Those who maintain that she was born in 1527 fail to consider or even ignore Gilbert Talbot's 1604 statement regarding Bess's age, that she was then 84; that her father provided funds for the upkeep of his daughters until each reached the age of 15; that she was espoused to Robert Barley in 1536; and, that she instigated her 1545/6 legal proceedings for her Barley dower as sole plaintiff.

The fact that at the likely time of their marriage ceremony (1543), Bess was some years older than 13-year-old Robert was neither unusual nor important. Bess's marriage to Robert had nothing to do with love in the modern sense. As with many marriages in the sixteenth century, it was a typical business transaction, a bargain, a result of the long-standing bonds between interrelated local and regional families of similar rank into which she was born. It was customary that on espousal the bride-to-be would go to live with the groom's family. There is a possibility that Bess was living with the Barleys from the time Ralph Leche and Arthur Barley agreed to Robert and Bess's spousal contract in 1536. We know she was not living at Hardwick in 1540.

Bess's mother, Elizabeth, would have overseen the education of her children. She wrote in a fine hand and would have passed skills such as that of household management onto her daughters who would have become skilled in things such as sewing, embroidery, brewing, baking, preparation of basic herbal medicines, the management of servants, and so forth. There is no evidence, that Bess and her sisters were taught various languages and other subjects that were certainly taught to high-born aristocratic ladies such as her granddaughter, Arbella. Bess's education would have been one appropriate to her rank.

Bess would have been brought up in the Catholic faith. Like Thomas Cromwell, the Greys, the Bayntons, and others of his circle, Sir William Cavendish came to favour evangelical Protestantism. Listed among his possessions at Northaw was an English Bible, probably Coverdale's 1539 Great Bible. Sir William St Loe, too, was a protestant. It may well have been during service in the Grey household that Bess was introduced to evangelical reform and turned away from the old religion. In her will, Bess speaks of the 'Elect', a term used predominately by Calvinists and Puritans. The Greys certainly had connections with continental reformers such as Bullinger and their daughter Jane received at least one letter from John Calvin.

In 1564, James Hardwick described Sir Francis Willoughby as his 'cousin' by which he meant close friend, not blood cousin. Yet no previous narrative of the Hardwicks has given sufficient weight to their connections with the Willoughbys of Wollaton and their servants, the Marmions. Bess herself first appears in the historical record in 1528 as an unnamed daughter in her father's will. In 1543/4, Peter Freschevile alleged that Bess's stepfather, mother, and family associate Henry Marmion, had forcibly abducted Robert Barley and that Bess's undated marriage to Robert was illegal. We have the complaint Bess made to Chancery in 1546 which gives some details of her marriage to Robert and of her efforts to secure dower.

If Bess did go into service within an aristocratic household following the death of her first husband, she would have witnessed the type of education received by noble children, especially if she was in service to the Greys. She would also become aware of the furnishings, tapestries, and trappings, typical of Tudor aristocratic households. A perusal of sixteen-century aristocratic household inventories readily demonstrates a propensity for French furniture, Turkey carpets, fine fabrics, hangings, and tapestries.

Bess's marriage to Cavendish introduced her to a wider circle of county families, some of high standing. It also provided her with a higher rank and the opportunity to become the mistress of a household, a role in which she could put into practice what she had imbibed. At this stage of her life, Bess was no more than the dutiful wife a man of Cavendish's rank and profession could expect. In his Star Chamber action against the 1548 enclosure riots, he referred to Bess only as 'my wife' and not by name, and he made no reference to her having at the time been some eight months pregnant with their first child. After all, having already fathered eight children pregnancy was nothing new to Sir William, he was no stranger to childbirth.

Bess's marriage to St Loe brought relief from the burden of Cavendish's debts together with the means to continue with the building of Chatsworth. We know from various inventories that Bess appears to have furnished properties in a fashion appropriate to her rank. We need to be cautious when ascribing any empathy or affinity she may or may not have had with styles, themes, or characters, as these would have been found in almost any aristocratic household of the Elizabethan Renaissance. In later life, Bess was happy to purchase preowned tapestries and to copy architectural features she had seen elsewhere.

Hardwick's new hall was originally intended to have had a double stairway but Bess appears to have abandoned this in favour of a grand winding staircase leading to the High Great Chamber after having seen that which Sir Christopher Hatton had installed at his magnificent house at Holdenby, Northamptonshire. The High Great Chamber frieze at Hardwick is a rare survival of Elizabethan architecture but William Cecil had such a frieze at Theobalds with trees so realistic it was said birds built their nests in them, a conceit that would have delighted the Elizabethans. We know that Bess's son Charles Cavendish saw this frieze.

The building of Hardwick's new hall had probably already extended above the height of the first floor when in 1592 Bess purchased Hatton's Gideon tapestries. Typically, the State Rooms of an Elizabethan prodigy house would be located on the first floor. I suspect that the height of the Gideon tapestries was too great for them to hang on the new hall's first floor. This led to a reversal of the norm with the State Rooms being placed on the second floor the height of which was constructed to accommodate the Gideon tapestries. In order to maintain the symmetry of the building, this necessitated the addition of a further mullion to Hardwick's lofty towers.

The death of Sir William Cavendish must have had a traumatic and lasting effect on Bess, not simply due to the loss of another husband but also due to the stress created by the situation in which she found herself. For the second time, she was on the cusp of destitution but now with six children to support. This may have been a significant turning point in her life.

Probable reluctance by her stepfather to receive her back into the family after Robert Barley's death, her legal battle for a dower from the Barley estate, and now facing renewed fears of potential destitution following the death of Sir William Cavendish may have driven her to crave greater financial security for herself and her children. She was fortunate to have a good friend in Sir William St Loe who came to her rescue. They had known each other for many years before they married. He was certainly not desperate for an heir as some have claimed. Had that been the case, following the death of his first wife Anne Baynton in 1549, he would have remarried long before he married Bess a decade later.

St Loe and Bess spent relatively little time together during their six years of marriage. I find it hard to accept the idea that Queen Elizabeth demanded his attendance at court merely to spite Bess—why should she? As a courtier with a very important role, St Loe would have been expected to attend court just as Sir William Cavendish had had to maintain a London residence to fulfil his duties as a senior civil servant. It can be doubted that there was ever any intention for St Loe and Bess to live together or, indeed, to have children. Modern notions of love and marriage have little place in Tudor England. The fact that St Loe entrusted his inheritance to Bess had more to do with the complete breakdown of his relationship with his brother than it had to do with Bess. Bess had managed to escape impending poverty and destitution and she would have been determined never to find either herself or any of her children in such straits in the future.

I do not believe that Bess harboured a nefarious determination to fleece each of her husbands in turn. My Bess was not a confidence trickster or a uniquely ambitious dynast. In Tudor England, many young women were married to men far older than themselves and thus frequently outlived their husbands by many years. Women of rank were expected to remarry on one or more occasions. Not doing so was considered to be a sin against the natural order.

An ambitious widow could use the wealth gained from one marriage to attract husbands of a higher rank. Take, as a typical example, Margaret Donnington, the daughter of a Middlesex gentry family. Margaret's first husband was Thomas Kitson, a successful London mercer. Her second husband was Sir Richard Long who was a member of Henry VIII's Privy Chamber. Her third and last husband was the Earl of Bath. Her son, Thomas Kitson, was the father of the Margaret Kitson who was the first wife of Bess's son Charles Cavendish.

I do not see Bess's marriage to George Talbot as particularly unusual for the period. It should not be seen as the culmination of a conscious life-long single-minded quest for a title. Bess's brother James greatly increased the size of the family estate at Hardwick but bankrupted himself in the process. He died in the Fleet Prison.

The years around the mid-1580s and mid-1590s appear the have been especially difficult ones for Bess. In 1583, Bess's son William purchased the Hardwick estate on his mother's behalf, a fortuitous purchase which came at a time when Bess's marriage to George Talbot had completely broken down. She had had to leave Chatsworth and needed to find a new home. This must have been another stressful period for Bess and may well have revived fears of debt and poverty. The execution of Mary, Queen of Scots, in February 1587 demonstrated the likely fate of anyone who posed a threat to Elizabeth's crown and that included Bess's granddaughter, Arbella. The death of the Earl of Leicester in 1588 deprived Bess of a powerful ally at court. The Earl of Essex's feigned attraction to Arbella, coupled with fear of plots against the crown, led to Bess and Arbella's final exclusion from court in 1592 by which time the Cecils had already begun their efforts to secure the throne for James VI of Scotland. Little wonder that Bess became so protective of her granddaughter.

The economic and social shifts that took place in Tudor England saw many members of the traditional aristocracy fall upon hard times as population increase, the dissolution of the monasteries, and debasement of the coinage, all helped drive inflation to previously unseen levels. At the same time many nobles saw their traditional incomes from rents fall behind. On the other hand, urban economic recovery saw fortunes amassed by members of the rising 'middling sort.' The large doweries the daughters of the urban *nouveau riche* could bring to a marriage made them attractive brides for hard-up nobles. Often being much younger than their new husbands, such women became widows more than once and were able to accrue personal fortunes and bring wealth to future marriages as coverture bearing wives.

During the sixteenth century, unprecedented inflation led many nobles to turn from the traditional ways of gaining their incomes from copyholds, long-term fixed rents, and entry fines to short-term leaseholds and rack-renting. In addition to marrying an heiress or wealthy widow many began the commercial exploitation of their estates and the resources they contained such as coal, iron, stone, timber, pasture for sheep and cattle, warrens and fishponds. Notable among these were George Talbot.

I have little doubt that over the centuries much has been attributed to Bess that rightly ought to have been credited to others. As already noted, her brother James did much to enlarge the Hardwick estate and its income. Her sons William and Charles would have learned much about estate management from George Talbot's example. Bess is often credited with building Chatsworth but work on the new house began c.1554. In 1555, Sir William was seeking to employ Sir John Thynne's plasterer to work for him in the summer of the following year on the yet to be completed interior of the hall at Chatsworth. Much of the construction of the building had been finished by the time of Sir William's death in 1557.

Further work does not seem to have recommenced until 1560 when in April Bess repeated Sir William's request to Thynne to assist her in the hiring of a plasterer. Marriage to Sir William St Loe not only brought about the waiving of much of Cavendish's debt to the crown it also provided the funds to kick-start building at Chatsworth.

The sixteenth century produced many outstanding women. To name Elizabeth I, Margaret Willoughby, Anne Stanhope, Elizabeth Brooke, Margaret Lennox, Lettice Knollys, Penelope Rich, the Cooke sisters, would serve only to scratch the surface, but all were products of their time. All were ambitious for their children. The two decades between widow Bess Barley becoming Lady Cavendish in 1547 and in 1567 when she entered the ranks of the Tudor high aristocracy as Countess of Shrewsbury demonstrates how a woman from the ranks of the lower gentry could rise through the ranks to the peak of the nobility.

Advances in women's history is increasingly bringing to light the stories of many Tudor women who rose from modest backgrounds to join the ranks of the higher Tudor aristocracy. The example of Margaret Donnington has already been noted. Vanessa Wilkie's 2023 biography of Alice Spencer offers another case in point, so much so that it is aptly titled *A Woman of Influence: The Spectacular Rise of Alice Spencer in Tudor England.* The niece of Charles Cavendish and Margaret Kitson, Alice became the Countess of Derby, and rose to become one of the most powerful women of her time.

My Bess was not unique. She is more human than is often portrayed. Subject to human frailties she was just as often at the mercy of events as she was controlling them. In February 1603, for the one and only time and in exceptional circumstances, she described her 53-year-old son Henry Cavendish as her 'bad sonne'; yet for her son-in-law, Gilbert Talbot, writing in 1604, she was his 'unkind mother-in-law'. My Bess was neither a *femme fatale*, proto-feminist or paragon of virtue. My Bess was simply a woman of her time.

Appendix

Among the subsidiary titles of the earls of Shrewsbury is that of Baron Talbot, a title which lapsed in 1616 on the death of Bess' son-in-law, Gilbert Talbot, 7th Earl of Shrewsbury. Gilbert is believed to have married Bess' daughter, Mary Cavendish, in February 1568. One of their places of residence was Staffordshire's Ingestre Hall which, rebuilt in 1613, today houses a portrait dated 1575 alleged to be of Elizabeth, Countess of Shrewsbury, *viz,* Bess of Hardwick.

Ingestre Hall Residential Arts Centre

Notwithstanding that the sitter appears to look rather young for a woman who in 1575 would have been well over fifty years of age, chapter five of this book demonstrates Bess' strong sense of rank and status. The Ingestre portrait bears heraldic arms surmounted by a baronial coronet. It seems highly unlikely that someone as acutely status conscious as Bess, who as the Countess of Shrewsbury in 1575, would have been content to have mere baronial arms included in her portrait. It seems much more likely that the portrait is not of Bess but of her daughter, Gilbert Talbot's wife, Mary (née Cavendish).

The March 1989 edition of *Country Life* magazine featured an article, *'Rechristenings at Hardwick'*, written by Alastair Laing. Laing points out that the practice of naming sitters on portraits did not become fashionable until the eighteenth-century and placing names on frames did not become common until the nineteenth-century. Hardwick inventories taken in 1792 and 1811 demonstrate that during this period many early portraits at Hardwick were mistakenly identified by the 5th Duke of Devonshire and so 'lost' their true identities. At that time at least four early sixteenth-century portraits were inscribed as being members of the Cavendish family, three of which have now been correctly identified. The National Trust currently and tentatively identify the fourth portrait as a posthumous portrait of Sir William Cavendish's grandfather, Thomas Cavendish (d1477), but this seems doubtful.

William Fitzwilliam, 1st Earl of Southampton. Although identified as
Sir Thomas More this portrait is almost certainly the portrait of the
Earl of Southampton listed in the 1601 Hardwick inventory.
© National Trust Images.

The 1792 inventory simply describes many portraits as being 'a portrait of a lady' or 'of a gentleman.' When the 5th Duke died in 1811, a new inventory was compiled. Several previously nameless portraits now had been given a specific identity and the sitter's name added to the portrait in an antique script intended to give the impression that the name of the sitter was painted at the same time as the portrait itself. Among these portraits is one inscribed 'Sir Thomas Moore'.

Neither the Northaw inventory of the 1540s, the Chatsworth inventories of 1553 (1559), the Hardwick inventories of 1601, or the eighteenth-century inventories, refer to a portrait of Sir Thomas More. We now know that the portrait inscribed Sir Thomas More is actually of Sir William FitzWilliam, 1st Earl of Southampton (c.1490-1542). The mis-identification of William FitzWilliam as Sir Thomas More begs the question as to whether or not there ever was a portrait of More in the first place. But why then would the 5th duke have thought that the FitzWilliam portrait was of Thomas More unless he believed that there was such a portrait?

Prior to 1792 the identity of the sitter in numerous Hardwick's portraits was handed down by word-of-mouth, often by successive housekeepers. In 1792 the portrait currently believed to be that of Thomas Cavendish (d.1477) was described as being of a 'Man, with a Black Cap, robe of Furr, Hands in the attitude of Prayer'. At the time, the sitter was thought to possibly be Erasmus. However, the portrait came to be identified and inscribed as 'Thomas Cavendish'. A close inspection reveals that the sitter is wearing

Thomas Cavendish?
National Trust Images

Sir Thomas More,
Hans Holbein,
© Phillip Mould Images

the typical scholar's cap of the early sixteenth-century, as worn by the likes of Erasmus, More and John Colet. It could very possibly be a 'lost' portrait of Sir Thomas More.

There will be those who object that to the right and left of the sitter there are two Cavendish heraldic devices that would identify the sitter as George Cavendish, not Sir Thomas More. However, these devices are now known to have been added to the portrait sometime between 1811 and 1860 and were not a feature of the original painting. The hands of the sitter appear to be positioned to suggest supplication and piety thus giving the portrait a religious overtone. To have mistaken the sitter as being Erasmus may not have been far wide of the mark.

The artist who painted the Hardwick portrait is unknown but suffice it to say it wasn't Hans Holbein. But, when compared to known portraits of Sir Thomas More,[*] a number of similarities can be discerned, not least his rather long, straight pointed nose !

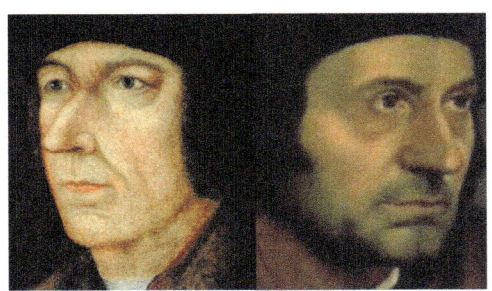

Hardwick's portrait may well be a 'lost' portrait of Sir Thomas More and it is possible that the house is the home of a portion of another 'lost' portrait. At the north-east end of the Long Gallery there is what, on a cursory look, appears to be simply a head and shoulder portrait of Henry VIII. However, on closer inspection, something doesn't look quite right. The portrait seems too big to fit the frame in which it sits. Each of the king's shoulders are cut off as is the intricate gold chain around them. An artist would be unlikely to paint his subject in this way, thus giving the impression that what was once a full-size portrait, which may have become damaged, has been cut to fit the frame. This is worthy of further investigation.

* See, for example, Portraits of Sir Thomas More [Paintings, Tudor images, pictures of saints] (www.luminarium.org)

Bibliography

Primary Sources:

Barlow, G. D. (1911) *Published Matter and Records relating to the Families of the Name Barlow*.

Barlow, Sir Montague, *Barlow Family Records, 1932*.

Bath Mss, Thynne Mss. 2, ff 250-253v

Belvoir Castle Muniments is a book of manuscript pedigrees of landed families c1565

Borthwick Institute for Archives, University of York, 17184384

will of John Marmyon of Cotgrave, October 1521. Vol. 9, f.180

Borthwick Institute for Archives, University of York, 17184908 will of Gabriel Barwick, 1570

Borthwick Institute for Archives, University of York, 17184976

Borthwick Institute for Archives, University of York,

Nottingham Act Book. Gabriel Marmion of Arnold, Admin, Jan 1590/1

Boynton, L. (1971) *The Hardwick Hall Inventories of 1601*.

Cecil Papers, vol 16, November 1604, Gilbert Talbot's letter to Robert Cecil confirming Bess's age, HMC

Clay J. W. (ed.) (1908) *North Country Wills; being abstracts of wills relating to the counties of York, Nottingham, Northumberland, Cumberland, and Westmorland, at Somerset House and Lambeth Palace 1383*.

Devonshire MSS, Chatsworth, Hardwick MSS 7, Account Book of Countess of Shrewsbury, 1591-97, fol. 195

Devonshire MSS, Chatsworth, H/143/6

Devonshire MSS, Chatsworth, Hardwick MS 29, 4

Devonshire MSS., Chatsworth, Hardwick MS 29, 16

Folger Shakespeare Library, Cavendish-Talbot MSS, X.d.428 (34) www.folgerpedia.edu.com

Foster, J. Grey's Inn Register of Admissions 1521-1889

Harvey, W. (ed.) 1565 Wiltshire Visitation, 1897

Johnson, N. (Unpublished) *Lives of the Earls of Shrewsbury*, unpublished MS Chatsworth.

Marshall, G. W. (ed.) (1623) *The Visitation of Wiltshire*.

Metcalfe, W. C. (ed.) (1891) *The Visitations of Derbyshire, 1569 and 1611*, Vol 7.

Nichols, J. G. (ed.) (1850) *The Chronicle of Queen Jane and Queen Mary* (Camden Society, Old Series 48).

Nichols, J. G. (ed.) (1857) *The Literary Remains of King Edward the Sixth*.

Northamptonshire Archives

FH 1320

FH 1702

Nottinghamshire Archives

DD/P/CD/113 - Arthur Barley, Statute of Uses

DD/P/114/10

157/DD/P/114/2 - Gabriel Marmion described as Bess's servant, 1576

157 DD/48/14

Records of the Honorable Society of Lincoln's Inn. Admissions and Chapel Registers, The Honourable Society of Lincoln's Inn, 1896.

Steen. S. J. (ed.) (1994) *The Letters of Lady Arbella Stuart.*

Stevenson, W. H. (1911) *Report on the manuscripts of Lord Middleton by Great Britain. Royal Commission on Historical Manuscripts; Middleton, Digby Wentworth Bayard Willoughby, baron, 1844-1922, HMC.*

Sturgess, H. A. C. (ed) (1949) *Register of Admissions to the Honourable Society of the Middle Temple.*

Thynne Papers, Longleat, TH/VOL/III/9 - Bess's seeks Sir John Thynne's help

Thynne Papers, Longleat, TH/VOL/III/11 - Bess thanks Sir John Thynne for his help

The National Archives at Kew (hereafter, TNA), C = Court of Chancery; CP Court of Common Pleas; PROB = Probate; STAC = Star Chamber; E=Exchequer; REQ= Court of Requests. See text footnotes for details.

TNA CP 40/1092

TNA CP 40/1096

TNA CP40/1120 - Abduction of Robert Barley; Elizabeth Barley, wife of Arthur, claim for dower

TNA CP40/1124

TNA CP40/1125 - Freschevile agrees to pay dower to Arthur Barley's widow
TNA CP40/1135 - Peter Freschevile, Recognisance
TNA C 21/B10/3
TNA C 43/2/34
TNA C 1/102/57-59
TNA C 1/1291/17-21
TNA C 1/430/18
TNA C 1/1365/5-7
TNA C 142/140/203
TNA C 142/21/35 - John Hardwick, senior, Inquisition Post-Mortem
TNA C 142/282/103
TNA C 142/35/31
TNA C 142/37/86
TNA C 142/68/51
TNA C 1/427/25
TNA C 146/7541
TNA C 146/11066
TNA C 241/282/103 - Henry Marmion, executor to John Hardwick's will
TNA C 1/519/55
TNA C 1/545/3
TNA C 1/546/53
TNA C 1/593/13
TNA C 1 845/34 - Bess's mother v Ralph Leche, desertion
TNA C 1/849/9
TNA C 1/852/27-31
TNA C 1/852/21-26
TNA C 1/860/14-15 - Henry Marmion purchase of Rebert Barley's wardship and marriage
TNA C 1/861/28
TNA C 1/1101/17 - Bess's complaint to Chancery, 1546
TNA C 1/1102/17
TNA C 1/1120/44
TNA C 1/1102/40
TNA C 1/1102/37-39 - 41 - Boswell's complaint against John Hardwick's executors
TNA C 2/Eliz/E2/36

TNA C 3/170/13(2)

TNA C 78/78/14

TNA C 78/33/34

TNA C 3/11/108 - George Barley's complaint for spoil

TNA E 40/547

TNA E 40/10747

TNA E 40/14639 - Marriage indenture, Henry Marmion

TNA E 101/424/10 - investigation into Sir William Cavendish's accounts

TNA E 150/1161/13 - Henry Marmion, Inquisition Post-Mortem

TNA E 150/743/8 - John Hardwick, Inquisition Post-Mortem and will, Jan 1528

TNA E 150/753/2

TNA E 150/554/11

TNA E 150/1127/8

TNA PROB 11/15/39 - will of Mauncer Marmion

TNA PROB 11/22/542 - will of Sir Henry Willoughby

TNA PROB 11/28/534 - will of Edward Marmion

TNA PROB 11/42B/241

TNA PROB 11/48/200 - will of Sir William St Loe

TNA PROB 11/48/395 - will of Thomas Leeke

TNA PROB 11/67/450 - will of Thomas Busby

TNA PROB 11/111/213 - Bess's will

TNA REQ 2/6/212

TNA STAC 2/7, ff 15-16 - Bugby's complaint re-attack on Hardwick

TNA STAC 2/17/53 - attack on Langley Close

TNA STAC 2/19/310 - Arthur Barley, Debt

TNA STAC 20/2/40, fol 1r - attack on Langley Close

TNA STAC 2/22/240

TNA STAC 2/22/359 - attack on Langley Close

TNA STAC 2/24/182

TNA STAC 2/25/327-328 - attempted arrest of Machell

TNA STAC 2/28/49

TNA STAC 2/33/4 - Machell incident

TNA STAC 2/37/4 - attempted arrest of Machell

TNA STAC 3/1/49 - Northaw Riots

TNA STAC 3/10/43

TNA STAC 4/1/7

TNA WARD 7/1/66 (no.164) - Arthur Barley, Inquisition Post-Mortem: Boswell's purchase of Robert Barley's wardship

TNA WARD 9/152 - Boswell's purchase of Robert Barley's wardship

University of Nottingham,

UNMASC Mi C15 - letter from William (?) Marmion 1583/4

UNMASC Mi C 15 - Marmion, servant of Elizabeth, Countess of Shrewsbury, to Sir Francis Willoughby, about quarrels between the countess and her husband, and referring to imprisonment of Mary, Queen of Scots c1570-1583

UNMASC Mi C23

UNMASC Mi 1/3/1-2

UNMASC Mi 2/77/102

UNMASC Mi 5/169/1/104

UNMASC Mi 5/169/1/108-109 - Licence to alienate: Sir Francis Willoughby to Anne Marmion, widow; Location: Arnold Nottinghamshire c 1594

UNMASC Mi 5/169/84, 85, 88 dated 1562

UNMASC, Mi 5/169/1/105 - Marriage indenture; Gab. Marmion, and Cowper and Eyre; Location: Arnold, Nottingham Nottinghamshire 3 June 1584

UNMASC, Mi 6/170/124/5

UNMASC Mi 6/175/46 - Will of Sir Henry Willoughby, 1528

UNMASC Mi 6/175/68 - Bundle of title deeds, legal papers and acquittances mostly relating to Inquisitions and wills of members of the Willoughby family 1510-1586

UNMASC Mi 6/176/190

UNMASC Mi 6/177/96

UNMASC, Mi 6/178/49

UNMASC Ne D 848.

Walpole, H. (1798) *The Works of Horatio Walpole, Earl of Orford,* IV.

Woolley collection Brit Mus Add Mss 6671; 'The Memorandum of Arthur Mower'

Secondary Sources:

Alford, S. (2013) *The Watchers: A Secret History of the Reign of Elizabeth 1.*

Ashead, D. and Taylor, D. A. H. B. (eds) (2016) *Hardwick Hall: A Great Old Castle of Romance.*

Beer, B. L. 'Edward, Duke of Somerset [known as Protector Somerset] (c500-1552)', *Oxford Dictionary of National Biography*

Beer, B L. (1973) *The Political Career of John Dudley, Earl of Warwick and Duke of Northumberland.*

Beer, B. L. (1979) 'Northumberland: the myth of the wicked duke and the historical John Dudley', *Albion*, 11.

Bindoff, S. T. (1892) *History of Parliament. Commons 1509-58*, 3 Vols.

Borman, T. (2018) 'Schemer, Social Climber … Scourge of Elizabeth I', *BBC History Magazine.*

Bradley. E. T. (2007) *Life of the Lady Arabella Stuart: Containing a Biographical Memoir and a Collection of Her Letters*, 2 vols.

Burke, B. (1884) *The Grand Armoury.*

Bush, M. L. (1975) *The Government Policy of Protector Somerset*, London: Edward Arnold.

Clay, Sir Charles, *Complete Peerage*, VIII.

Collinson, P. (1987) *The English Captivity of Mary, Queen of Scots*, Sheffield History Pamphlets.

Coss, P. 'Robert Marmion (d. 1144)' (2004) *Oxford Dictionary of National Biography.*

Cressy, D. S. (1999) *Birth, Marriage & Death: Ritual, Religion, and the Life-Cycle in Tudor and Stuart England.*

Collins, A. (1752) *Historical Collections of the Noble Families of Cavendish, Holles, Vere, Harley and Ogle.*

Coward, B. (1988) *Social Change and Continuity in Early Modern England, 1550-1750.*

Cruz, A. M. (2019) *An Account of an Elizabethan Family: The Willoughbys of Wollaton*, Camden Series.

Davey, R. (1912) *The Sisters of Lady Jane Grey and their Wicked Grandfather.*

Dugdale, Sir William (1675) *The Baronage of England.*

Durant, D. N. (1978) *Arbella Stuart: A Rival to the Queen.*

Durant, D. N. (1999) *Bess of Hardwick: Portrait of an Elizabethan Dynast.*

Durant, D. N. (2011) *The Smythson Circle.*

Durant, D. N. and Riden, P. (eds) (1984) *The Building of Hardwick Hall, 'Part 2', The New Hall, 1591-98*, Derbyshire Record Society 9.

Flower, A. (2007) *Tudor Women's Legal Rights, 1485-1603.*

Gammon, S. R. (1973) *Statesman and Schemer: William First Lord Paget, Tudor Minister.*

Girouard, M. (1966) *Robert Smythson and the Architecture of the Elizabethan Era.*

Goldring, E. (2004) 'Talbot, Elizabeth [Bess of Hardwick], Countess of Shrewsbury (1527-1608)' *Oxford Dictionary of National Biography.*

Goldring, E. (2004) 'Talbot, George, sixth Earl of Shrewsbury (c1522-1590)', *Oxford Dictionary of National Biography.*

Gristwood, S. (2003) *Arbella: England's Lost Queen,* Bantam Books.

Gunn, S. (2015) *Charles Brandon: Henry VIII's closest friend.*

Hardy Blanche, C. (1913) *Arbella Stuart: A Biography,* Kessinger Publishing.

Haselwood, F. (1875) *The Genealogy of the Family of Haselwood: Wickwarren, Belton and Maidwell Branches.*

Hoak, D. E. (1976) 'Rehabilitating the duke of Northumberland: politics and political control, 1549-53", in Loach and Tittler (eds), *The Mid-Tudor Polity*

Hoak, D. E. *The King's Council in the Reign of Edward VI.*

Hubbard. K. (2018) *Devices & Desires: Bess of Hardwick and the Building of Elizabethan England.*

Hurstfield, J. (1971) *Elizabeth I and the Unity of England.*

Ives, E. W. (1986) *Anne Boleyn.*

Ives, E. W. (2011) *Lady Jane Grey: a Tudor Mystery.*

Jones, A. C. 'Commotion Time: The English risings of 1549' (Unpublished PhD thesis, University of Warwick, 2003).

Jordan, W. K. (1968) *Edward VI: the young king.*

Kilburn, T. (2016) 'Three Into Two Won't Go: Hardwick's Eglantine Table', Derbyshire Archaeological Society, *Derbyshire Miscellany,* Vol. 21, Part 2.

Kilburn, T. (2014) 'The Wardship and Marriage of Robert Barley, First Husband of Bess of Hardwick', *Derbyshire Archaeological Journal,* Vol. 134.

Kilburn, T. (2016) 'The Wardship and Marriage of Robert Barley: An Addendum', *Derbyshire Archaeological Journal,* Vol. 136.

Kilburn, T. (2019) 'Sir William Cavendish: Marriage to Bess and Relocation to Derbyshire', *Derbyshire Archaeological Journal,* Vol. 139.

Kilburn. T. (2023) *Young Bess: The Early Years of Bess and Her Sisters,* JetPrint, Whitby.

Kilburn. T. (2023) *My Bess,* JetPrint, Whitby.

Kingsford, C. L. (ed.) (1910) 'Two London chronicles from the collections of John Stowe', *Camden Miscellany,* 4, Camden Society, 3rd ser, 18.

Laing, A. (1989) 'Rechristenings at Hardwick', *Country Life,* 183.

Loach, J. (1999) *Edward VI.*

Loach, J. and Tittler, R. (eds) (1980), *Problems in Focus: The Mid-Tudor Polity, c.1540-1560.*

Loades, D. M. (1989) *Mary Tudor.*

Lodge, E. (1838) *Illustrations of British History.*

Lovell. M. S. (2006) *Bess of Hardwick, First Lady of Chatsworth.*

MacCulloch, D. (2018) *Thomas Cromwell: A Life.*

Maddison, A. R. (1902) *Lincolnshire Pedigrees.*

Malkiewicz, A. J. A. (1955) 'An eye-witness's account of the coup d'etat of October 1549', *English Historical Review,* 70.

McElroy. A., *Women's Lives in the Tudor Era*, Pen & Sword, Barnsley, 2024

Merton, C. I. (1991) *The Women Who Served Queen Mary and Queen Elizabeth: Ladies, Gentlewomen and Maids, 1553-1603*, PhD Thesis, Trinity College, Cambridge University. Cam.ac.uk

Neale, J. E. (1979) *Queen Elizabeth 1.*Norrington, R. (2002) *In the Shadow of the Throne.*

North, J. (ed) (2005) *England's Boy King: the diary of Edward VI, 1547-1553.*

Palmer, C. F. R. (1875) *History of the Baronial Family of Marmion.*

Paul, J. (2022) *The House of Dudley.*

'Pedigree of the Freschevile and Musard Families', *Collectanea Topographica et Genealogica*, 4, 1837.

Pollard, A. F. (1900) *England Under Protector Somerset.*

Riden, P. (2006) 'Bess of Hardwick and the St Loe Inheritance' in P. Riden and D. G. Edwards (eds), *Essays in Derbyshire History Presented to Gladwyn Turbutt* (Derbyshire Record Society, 30).

Riden, P. (2009) 'Sir William Cavendish: Tudor civil servant and founder of a dynasty', *Derbyshire Archaeological Journal,* 129.

Riden. P. (2010) 'The Hardwicks of Hardwick Hall in the Fifteenth and Sixteenth Centuries', *Derbyshire Archaeological Journal,* 130.

Riden, P. and Fowkes, D. (2009) *Hardwick a great house and its estate.*

Scard, M. (2016) *Edward Seymour, Lord Protector: Tudor King in all but name.*

Skidmore, C. (2007) *Edward VI: the lost king of England.*

Summerson, M. (2004) 'Robert Marmion (d. 1216-18)', *Oxford Dictionary of National Biography.*

Stone, L. (1979) *Family, Sex and Marriage.*

Stone, L. (1979) *The Crisis of the Aristocracy, 1558-1641.*

White, J. (2005) '"That whycheysnedefoulle and nesesary": the nature and purpose of the original furnishing and decoration of Hardwick Hall' (Unpublished PhD thesis, University of Warwick).

Wilson, V. (1922) *Queen Elizabeth's Maids of Honour*.

Wright, S. M. (1983) *The Derbyshire Gentry in the Fifteenth Century*.

Index

171

Printed in Great Britain
by Amazon

48226355R00099